THE ART OF BECOMING A
MULTIMILLIONAIRE
Real Estate Investor

**A Step-By-Step Guide
to Achieving Real
Estate Success**

MIKE and TOLLA CHERWENKA

BLUEPRINT PRESS
INTERNATIONALE

The Art of Becoming a Multimillionaire Real Estate Investor
Copyright © 2023 by Mike and Tolla Cherwenka

ISBN
978-1-961117-44-0 (Paperback)
978-1-961117-45-7 (eBook)
978-1-961117-43-3 (Hardcover)

To our parents, Mike and Ilse Cherwenka and Gilberto and Laurine Soto, for their unconditional love, support, and inspiration.

TABLE OF CONTENTS

WHAT INDUSTRY LEADERS ARE SAYING ABOUT MIKE AND TOLLA CHERWENKA

We have been waiting twenty years to learn the detailed secrets from the "Godfather of Fix-and-Flip" and the "First Lady of Real Estate."
—David Stallings, HomeStar Financial

Mike and Tolla recovered from the real estate crash using these simple, step-by-step instructions.
—Bryan Stone, *The Real Estate Connection*, radio talk show host

This is an easy read! Practical lessons that will benefit both naive investors and skilled professionals.
—Rock Shukoor, Atlanta Freedom Club, author, coach, and mentor

Mike and Tolla revitalized the most distressed areas in Atlanta and appreciated values. True pioneers!
—Mark Blumstein, secured investment lending

What every real estate investor needs to know about financing with little or no money, wholesaling, rehabbing, staging, and selling.
—Jack Kudron, veteran real estate investor

Mike has fixed and flipped more homes than anyone in the industry. He's known as the Godfather, so you're learning from a seasoned veteran.
—Bill Preston, owner, Air Conditioning Experts

Mike Cherwenka is one of the most successful single-family real estate investors in the Atlanta metro area. Many of us know him as the "Godfather of Wholesaling Houses," but he is so much more. Mike is a true mover, shaker, and deal maker. He knows the real estate game inside and out and plays at a very high level. He's now "flipping the hood" with his lovely and highly talented wife, Tolla, and they are literally transforming blighted communities into beautiful neighborhoods one house at a time. And when Mike leads, others follow since everything he touches turns to gold. When Mike talks, people listen and you should, too. Read Mike's book, get to know him, watch him, and you too can discover your own gold mine in real estate investing and make millions like Mike.

—Dustin Griffin, Executive Director
Atlanta Real Estate Investors Alliance (AtlantaREIA.com)

Over the past fifteen-plus years, I've seen firsthand their impressive perseverance and success, and now these industry secrets are available in an accessible, step-by-step format for investors to attain their own success.

—Andrea Clayton Executive Administrative Assistant,
Cherwenka Team

MEET THE CHERWENKAS

Our ministry is real estate, and we strongly believe that we were placed on this earth to give of ourselves in this capacity. God has blessed us, and His blessings are abundant in our lives.

Mike Cherwenka is known as the "Godfather of Fix-and-Flip" because he has flipped more than 2,100 homes. Mike also fosters real estate investors on their journeys to becoming experienced investors. He has a philosophy of teaching through a hands-on flipping experience.

Mike and his wife, Tolla Cherwenka, started flipping luxury homes in upscale communities in Atlanta, Georgia, in 2005. Additionally, Tolla is a worldwide thought leader and business-transformation architect for a Fortune 500 software company.

While giving interviews on various media outlets and at events, people have constantly asked us to write a book to help them in their real estate investor journeys. This book serves as a step-by-step, easy-to-follow process on the key items to focus on when renovating a home for huge profit.

MIKE'S STORY

I transitioned into real estate investing on April 15, 1996. I bought my first foreclosure property, and the following month I bought two more that needed total rehabbing. Well, anything that could go wrong did:

The wholesaler, who was a hard money lender too, falsified after-repair value (ARV) or estimates. Simply defined, ARV is what a property will be worth when the rehab is complete. He didn't provide the additional funds for cost overruns as agreed. The contractors cheated me. Every time I had a property under contract, it fell through.

In December 1996, if it had cost fifty cents to travel around the world, I couldn't have afforded to get out of sight. God did not intervene before I became completely broke. I hadn't made a dime in twelve months, and debt was growing rapidly each day.

I was shocked at my downfall because I thought God would bless me economically since I gave up a lucrative career and just walked out in faith. Instead of eating caviar on my yacht as I planned, I was sleeping at the properties, fixing up properties with no utilities, taking, showers at the truck stop, working fourteen hours hard labor each day waiting for another credit card application to come in the mail so I could get through another month.

One night I was alone in a property, battling my anger, sorrow, and self-pity. I was awakened by two huge trees that fell on both sides of the house. Both trees were split in half, but they did not hit either of the properties that I was working on. There was no other storm damage in the area. At that moment, I realized that God was responding to my cries the night before.

In the photo above, before Mike was saved from sin, Mike ran the one of the most successful male reviews that went on the international fame.

Prior to becoming a real estate investor, I owned and was the featured dancer in an internationally famous show. During those seven years of dancing, sin and I were good friends. I was on countless talk shows Donahue, Sally Jessie Raphael, Montel Williams, Joan Rivers, Jerry Springer, *Real Sex*, and more. Check out this brief footage from Joan Rivers's show, https://youtu.be/z4BAlOQgtfk.

That shot me to a level of fame, power, and success unimaginable to most. In early 1995, at the top of my career, I walked out onto the stage. The lights were bright, the music was pounding, but God was binding me. There I stood, locked in place, embarrassingly naked and confused about the loss of joy. After that incident, I made a clean break from dancing. However, I left the environment, but I didn't completely remove the environment from me.

God split those trees because he needed me to make a full transition into the likeness of him, so I cut my long, curly dancing hair; I sold all the jewelry that made me look like Mr. T's brother, and I divorced myself from bad relationships. As I took the stripper out of me, God was pouring his protection into me.

Twenty years later, I have flipped over two thousand homes and profited more than $15 million. In recent years, various real estate associations have crowned me the "Godfather of Wholesaling Real Estate"; it's actually a name I take great pride in as I use my relationship with God to empower others.

TOLLA'S STORY

When most six-year-olds were playing with dolls or playing kickball with their friends, I spent my free time hacking computers and memorizing articles to amuse my family with my ability to photographically recall whatever content I consumed.

My venture into the world of IT started because my father returned home after being deployed abroad for a while. They said that when he came home, I was terrified of him because I didn't recognize him. That tore my dad's heart up. So he became obsessed with recreating a connection with me. While reestablishing our bond, my dad noticed that I had unique attractions to his army-issued computer. On a hunch, in 1977, my dad purchased and put a Commodore 65 computer in my room. After a few hacking incidents and mind-boggling algorithms I created, my dad sold me out to the Department of Defense.

At the age of fifteen, I was employed to write algorithms to catch military personnel and their families stealing rations. (When military families are deployed, the family may have a monthly maximum that they can spend on items from the commissary and other on-base retailers.) When those criminals were busted black marketing by the military, I was the kid in the back room catching them.

While attending high school in Seoul, Korea, a classmate approached me about taking my photo for his mom, who was a modeling agent. It was raining and humid the day he took the picture, so I looked like a Q-tip in the photo (skinny body and bog hair), and I didn't hear from his mom. A few months later, I was leaving school when my friend's mom walked by and saw me. She jumped out of her car and offered a modeling job. That was the opening to the world of entertainment for me. I went to be in movies, TV shows, and commercials in Korea and the United States.

Here is a clip from my very first movie: https://www.youtube.com/watch?feature=youtu.be&v=QTfwBYzYReA&app=desktop.

My modeling and engineering careers were on the rise. A bigger agency offered me a job modeling in Paris. My dad was all for it, but my mom said it was the dumbest thing that she'd heard of. She told me that God had blessed me with an amazing brain, so why would I throw it away on a superficial feature. I was so mad at her, but in hindsight, I see she was right! I had my dad work on her, but it was to no avail, so at seventeen years old, I headed back to the United States to start my college career. I actually graduated high school at sixteen years old, but my parents did not let me go off to college to early because they said that I was too naive.

When I was nineteen years old, I started working as an aerospace engineering consultant for the Lockheed Martin Marietta C-130J first flight team. Our work revolutionized the aerospace and automotive industry.

After marrying at a very young age, I was blessed with two beautiful girls, Olivia and Lauren Clay, aka "Noodle" and "Toodle," respectively.

In 2002, I moved into a house that was two doors down from Mike's house. At the time, he was married, and I was in a long-term relationship.

Although I was a single mom, I was able to buy an eight-thousand-square-foot house with the profits from my IT consulting company. Additionally, because I clearly didn't have enough to do, I opened a hair salon that was highly successful for ten years. While I was running my IT consulting company, the largest hair salon in the Southeast, I obtained a real estate license.

In 2003, Mike and I decided to start building homes, townhouses, and multimillion-dollar homes on Lake Lanier. We were raking in the money until that bottom fell out in 2007.

During the downturn, Mike started day-trading, and I focused exclusively on IT. Today, I flip houses with Mike, run our real estate brokerage team, and work as a worldwide thought leader and business-transformation architect, helping business stakeholders—executives to end-users—in large-scale organizations develop and implement strategic plans, align business to IT, optimize enterprise assets, and reduce operating costs. I provide companies with industry's best thinking, problem solving, and innovation in Cloud, IOT, Digital, Agile IT, PMO, Enterprise Asset Modeling and Optimization, IT Governance, BI and IT Performance, DevOps, and PMO.

I have vast international and multicultural experiences, having worked and lived in the United States, Mexico, Korea, Germany, Ireland, Kuwait, Bahrain, Dubai and Canada led large teams in Asia and the Middle East and spent time visiting my clients across the globe.

I'm looking forward to providing guidance from a different perspective than Mike. While he is providing the guidance to help you transition to working for yourself full-time in real estate, I will provide the guidance to you keep your nine-to-five while building wealth.

MIKE AND TOLLA'S STORY

Because most people unknowingly focus on color not character, no one would have ever put us together, including us. Mike had Hugh Hefner tastes, that is, big, blue eyes, big, blonde hair, and big boobs. Tolla dated tall, dark, and handsome. Both of us were getting nowhere chasing what we wanted. Independent of each, both we realized that we had to turn our love lives over to God.

In 2012, while participating in an annual Feeding the Hungry event, a man walked up to Tolla to thank her for the food that she and her friend had packed up and brought down. Then he said, "People bring us food. But they don't think about bringing men anything to keep them warm, so I would appreciate whatever you can do." That man words inspired Tolla to do more. Two weeks later, she organized a coat-and-blanket charity drive. Although she hadn't spoken to Mike in five years, it was in her spirit to invite him to the coat drive. Fifteen minutes prior to the event ending, Mike showed up with a car loaded with brand-new jackets, coats, and clothes for men. The moment Mike walked in the door with an amazing smile and a spirit of giving, Tolla knew that God was positioning him for her. Mike knew that God sent him to her.

When we got engaged, we were the talk of the city. Whether it was the gym, walking around in our neighborhood, or grocery shopping, we would get speculative looks. After we were cornered in the grocery store by the nosiest neighbor in our hood, we decided to send out a press release (that's on the following pages) to feed our hungry community.

Friends, Family, and Business Associates,

On Saturday, May 18, Tolla Carlita Soto accepted my marriage proposal.

The love, respect, and chemistry between us is something I have never experienced. The nine-year journey of being divorced has finally come to a close. Tolla and I have a long history together, starting back in 2003 when she lived two doors down. She was the truest friend and like a little sister to me, although we never engaged in a romantic way. Our past friendship cemented the confidence of the true character and integrity I was looking for in a spouse.

I am honored to share our Celebration of Love with you.

Tolla is an IBM Senior Enterprise Architect, blessed with two lovely daughters Olivia-18 and Lauren-15 and lives in Inman Park.

Tolla wanted to share her thoughts:

> John 3:16—For God so loved the world that he gave his one and only Son, that whoever believes in him shall not perish but have eternal life.

Several years ago, God informed me of a transformational journey that I had to go through so that my wants and desires would decrease to enable the Holy Spirit to increase. He was very clear that I would battle many weapons that have been formed because I needed the battle wounds for my testimony and growth.

Most importantly, he told me to be still and wait for a man who would arrive in the likeness him. On November 25, 2014, God told me to go perform charity in his name, and he identified the participants he wanted me to invite. Unknown to me, on December 1, 2013, God sent the love of my life through the door fifteen minutes prior to the conclusion of the charity event. He immediately placed an immediate and different feeling on my spirit that caused me to look at my friend and former neighbor in a romantic and eternal light.

Saturday, May 18 Mike Cherwenka, my first love and the man God has been preparing me for, asked me for my hand in marriage.

During our whirlwind, Mike often said that he knew that he was moving in God's favor because God kept showing him 3:16 during moments of reflection or daily activity. In recognition of Mike's favorite biblical verse and the indications God gave him that he is walking in the light on the journey to eternal life, we are becoming one through God's will on 3:16/2014.

Mike & Tolla

CHAPTER 1

Mike and Tolla's Roles in the Wholesale Fix-and-Flip Process

I woke up one morning thinking about wolves and realized that wolf packs function as families. Everyone has a role, and if you act within the parameters of your role, the whole pack succeeds, and when that falls apart, so does the pack.

—Jodi Picoult

Amazingly, our greatest accomplishments and victories were on the heels of our greatest adversity. We have been broke, rich, broke, stupid rich, and stupid broke; however, the bad times didn't break us. During the 2007–2012 economic collapse, many seasoned investors were broken or left with a fraction of their previous fortunes. At the peak of the collapse, we constantly heard about people committing suicide because they thought the market would never come back. Others left the industry permanently.

We lost everything in the collapse. It was time for us to decrease so that God could increase in preparation for the new blessings that were coming our way. When everyone was saying the market was not back, God was empowering us with the confidence that it was back and to act now! We stepped out on faith and started buying homes at a strategic pace. It was time for our territory to expand.

Now Jabez was more honorable than his brothers, and his mother called his name Jabez, saying, "Because I bore him in pain." And Jabez called on the God of Israel saying, "Oh, that You would bless me indeed, and enlarge my territory, that Your hand would be with me, and that You

1

would keep me from evil, that I may not cause pain!" So God granted him what he requested (1 Chronicles 4:9–10).

Ask for God's blessing and then move in faith. To obtain our increased territory, we are working in the following roles in the real estate transaction.

- Skin-In Wholesaler
- Rehabber
- Stagers
- Real Estate Agents

For each of these roles, we will discuss throughout this book the activities in a step-by-step process that make us successful. Buckle up as we take you on an easy-to-read ride to building your real estate wealth.

🦶

Step One—Get Focused

CHAPTER 2

How to Get Focused

Perhaps the world isn't giving you what you want because based on all your distractions and lack of discipline it's unclear what you are asking for.

—Brendon Burchard

Many of us feel stuck. We're powerlessly trapped, doing things that aren't in our passions, but we feel as though we have to or we should do these things. Fear has us bound in invisible chains. When our goals aren't reached or even attempted, frustration and confusion set in.

A goal is a result that a person expects to achieve from effort; it is the desired target of an aim. Goal and purpose are synonyms.

Pause for a moment.

If you haven't accomplished your true goals, then you've accomplished your true purpose.

No goal/purpose in sports, business, or life happens when fears (weaknesses) are not identified and addressed. Fear has a way of masking itself beneath anger, frustration, confusion, and pain. Emotions control your life instead of fueling it. Dreams get deferred because you're poisoning and leading your brain to a slow and regrettable death by focusing on what you fear the most.

To stop the poisoning and slow brain death, focus on the pleasure you will receive from making the changes and taking actions and getting results. Dreaming is an important first step in becoming your agent of change. Dream about how your life will look after your goals have been accomplished. Picture buying your first investment house or multifamily residence to flip or rent, the rehab process, the person who will buy it. And most importantly, envision yourself at the closing receiving that first check or the day the rental agreement is signed. You will convert your dreams into beliefs by becoming confident in your ability to make them a reality.

Please do not continue to read without writing down the reasons that you have not started investing in real estate. On the left, write down your fears and on the right, write down your weaknesses. Use white space or extra paper if needed.

_____ _____

_____ _____

_____ _____

_____ _____

_____ _____

_____ _____

_____ _____

Those lines contain the fear and your perceived weaknesses that are stopping your beliefs from forming. Each word represents how you are allowing your goals/purpose to become unobtainable. When God calls you home, your greatest fears will become your greatest regrets.

Don't allow fear to prevent the changes that you need to obtain the results that you want. Imagine how your life will be if you continue to allow those fears to permanently chain you to your current state and miss your true purpose, your fear of a possible painful outcome.

To defeat fear, you must embrace the pain that may come when you make the changes that are needed. What do we mean? Like some people who can't lose weight because they focus on the daily pain from the small action steps that are needed to get the desired body in their dream. To obtain their goal weight, they should focus on the person they envision becoming. Those small action steps will no longer seem so insurmountable, because the vision in your mind is larger.

If you don't make the incremental changes, you will pretty much be that same old man or women that you have always been. You ever run into high school or college friends that you haven't seen in a while, and they are the same old person, not too much wiser and holding on to yesterday? Even worse, when you're connecting with old colleagues and friends, and they are *not* saying, "Wow! You have changed" or "You just keep getting better." If they are not saying that, we have news for you: you most likely are not growing and changing for the better. Fear prevents change. Another way to look it: when you allow fear to stop you from making the changes that are needed to put you in action daily to get the goals that you're aiming for, then you are allowing the greatest weapon of the devil to keep you chained to him. If you're not a believer, fear is the Jeffery Dahmer, American serial killer and cannibal, of your mind and spirit. You can allow him access to do his evil will or secure your territory from fear by fortifying it with impenetrable fences of belief.

We want to help you get stronger and more confident in obtaining your goals. Before you can make the changes needed to move forward, we must have a funeral and birth. It is time to kill off the person inside you who prevents you from making the changes needed to take action. For example, Tolla will tell who she used the *funeral-and-birth method.*

When I wanted to change the type of man I attracted, I created a list of the behaviors that I wanted to end in my life. It's my belief that you attract what you put out there as bait; meaning, if you want a faithful Christian, get a genuine relationship with God. If you want someone who is fit, work out. If you want unconditional love, love unconditionally. After I completed my list, I stood in front of a mirror, recited the list, created the shotgun motion with my arms, and then "shot" the old me. The visual of that experience is indelibly etched in my mind. I stopped focusing on those things that I didn't want to do. After all, I'd shot, killed, and buried the person inside me who had the behaviors that were preventing me from having what I wanted. Don't get me wrong. The murder scene wasn't and isn't a onetime fix. I focus daily on ensuring that old person does not return to me from the dead.

I prayed for daily strength too. Then the next person that God sent to me was Mike. As a married woman, I still focus and identify things that I need to change to achieve the results that I want. I implemented the *funeral-and-birth method* when I decided to

- go back to school at thirty-five to become an architect;
- lose thirty-five; and
- get my real estate license.

A rebirth started to happen because I spent more time focusing on what I wanted and taking action steps to make the changes that I needed to obtain the results I'd often envisioned in my dreams.

We want you to move past each fear by using it as fuel to spring into action. The brain is the most powerful organ. To get your daily task done, eighty-five billion neurons in the brain must complete upward of five trillion chemical reactions each second, at speeds of over two hundred sixty miles per hour. Your brain needs the fuel that you can extract from your emotions to drive your body and spirit to your dream destination. To transform those emotions that are hiding fears into fuel for your brain, you must line the path the neurons take with words of power.

Audit your thoughts often. Don't allow negativity to exist for long. When those negative thoughts penetrate your mind, swiftly flood your thoughts with gratitude, affirmation, and belief. Let's take step one in getting the fuel for your mind. Write down three power words that describe who you are.

_____ _____ _____

For example: unstoppable, determined, optimistic

Now let's turn those power words into one or a few sentences that will become your daily affirmation in the mirror. The following are Mike's and Tolla's, respectively.

> Thank you, God, for giving me favor in my life. I feel your blessings shining on me. I can certainly see my territory expanding all around me. I am ten feet tall and bulletproof.

> I am a daughter of a king. I will not be denied. All things are possible; I am determined. My day is full of opportunity.

After you recite your affirmation daily in the mirror, you will start to believe it. The chains will be broken as you continue to grow from your rebirth. To continue strengthening your focus, immerse yourself in the environment that will serve as the womb for your transformation. As you immerse yourself in the real estate womb of learning, it's going to get comfortable, warm, and safe. Like a baby who doesn't take action to exit the womb can die from lack of blood flow when it stays in too far beyond its due date, you can drown in the learning womb if you don't take action to quickly implement what you learn. It's imperative to learn and do. Don't become so smart with information from the learning womb that you overthink and overanalyze. Did you know that some of the most intelligent people in the world are least likely to take action on what they know?

It's going to take small and iterative actions to achieve your investing goals. What do we mean when we say immerse yourself in the real estate environment and do? Let's use some non-real-estate examples to make the point. If you want to become more positive, hang around positive people; then audit your words and thoughts often to ensure that you're delivering messages of positivity. If you want to lose weight, hang with people who have healthy diets; then take the action steps daily to remove the bad food and add more body movements each day. Immerse in the environment you want to be in so it can absorb into your mind and spirit. Act on the lesson from the new environment with positive thoughts, words, and actions. With effort, you will see a shift in your pain and pleasure sensors. Those bad things will no longer be good to you. Once your mind identifies your new environment as pleasurable, your focus will intensify. Confidence will show up in your life as knowledge, and taking action increases because fear will be decreasing.

The most imperative part of focus is daily action that projects you toward your real estate investing goals. For instance, when we tell you how to get started in real estate with no money, then you must do those actions to reach your goal of a first deal or expanding your existing investment portfolio.

Be encouraged by the decision you made to make real estate your path to achieving your envisioned dreams. When you're done reading this book, we will help you break through fear by providing you with priceless information and helping you develop an actionable plan to obtain your goals. We have our hands in various areas of real estate investing, but we're focusing this book on fix-and-flip and buy/hold (rental).

Other things to do as you develop an unstoppable focus, make better choices like filter out the time-eaters that are optional, like social networking, clubbing, TV watching. Spend time on activities that are moving you forward each day. Learn to know the difference between what's important and what isn't.

Be a better person. Arrive in the room and say, "Hey, there you are" not here I am. Then connect to each person you meet. Whether you a believer or not, you can't deny that love is the most powerful emotion that has been bestowed uniquely upon humans. Give with an open heart to others. When you get that first check from that rehab, walk into the closing room with a spirit of humility and gratitude.

TOP SECRET

Dreams, daily goals, and actions are oxygen to your real estate investment plans.

Focus on the actions that we're providing below to achieve your wealth-building dreams. To become more focused each day, make these actions a part of your *daily* routine:

- Develop a meditation plan.
- Set your goals.
- Pay attention to doing one thing at a time.
- Review what goals you accomplished at the end of the day.
- Practice arguing against yourself. Be your own "devil's advocate."
- Draw your vision of an ideal life or an ideal outcome to a specific situation.
- Update priorities.
- Talk to people who believe in you and your purpose.
- Read stories of success.

We commit thirty minutes each day to read, meditate, pray, review the previous day's accomplishments, and set goals. Our twenty-five-minute getting-focused activities are as follows:

- Fifteen minutes of morning devotion and prayer. We read Joel Osteen's morning devotions.
- Five minutes of review of the previous day's accomplishments, goal sharing.
- Five minutes of quiet self-reflection—set personal goals and action plans for the day's activities.

We block out time in the morning to ensure we run at the highest efficiency. We could have conversations at great length, but we know that discussion without action is just dreaming.

Action Step: Identify a room in your house where you can get into the focused _____.

Personal Financial Statement

Name:

Assets	Amount in Dollars
Cash—checking accounts	$ - 0
Cash—savings accounts	- 0
Certificates of deposit	- 0
Securities—stocks/bonds/mutual funds	- 0
Notes & contracts receivable	- 0
Life insurance (cash surrender value)	- 0
Personal property (autos, jewelry, etc.)	- 0
Retirement funds (e.g., IRAs, 401k)	- 0
Real estate (market value)	- 0
Other assets	- 0
Other assets	- 0
Total Assets	$ - 0

Liabilities	Amount in Dollars
Current Debt (Credit cards, accounts)	$ - 0
Notes payable	- 0
Taxes payable	- 0
Real estate mortgages	- 0
Other liabilities	- 0
Other liabilities	- 0
Total Liabilities	$ - 0
Net Worth	$ - 0

Before we proceed further, let's check your financial health. You may not be as bad off as you think!

Capture the problems that are preventing you from meeting your real estate investing goals. Use the problem-solving mind map on the following page to make positive action happen.

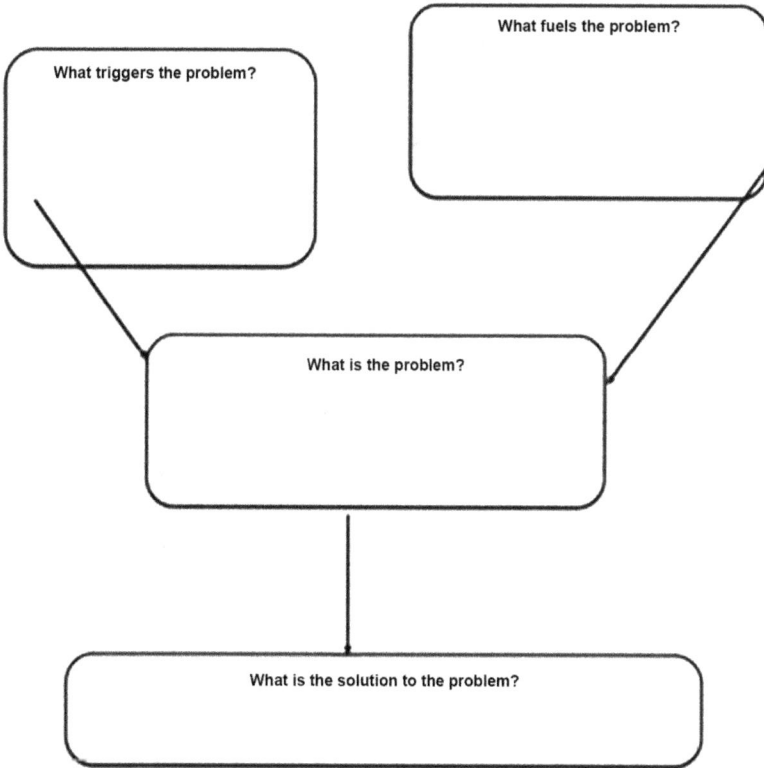

What fuels the problem?

What triggers the problem?

What is the problem?

What is the solution to the problem?

To Do	Doing	Done

Step Two—Get Money

CHAPTER 3

Understanding Credit

Friendship, like credit, is highest when it is not used.

—Elbert Hubbard

Credit Basics

Great credit is the foundation for long-term real estate success. If you have great credit that's awesome. Keep doing what you're doing. Most of us have room to improve our scores, bad to average, average to good, and so on.

The most common scoring models have a range of 300 to 850. Each lender sets its own standards for what constitutes a "good" score:

- 300–629: Bad credit
- 630–689: Fair credit, also called "average credit"
- 690–719: Good credit
- 720 and up: Excellent credit

Most hard money lenders a require a 620 score or better.

TOP SECRET

It's important to note that repairing bad credit is a like losing weight: it takes time, and there is no quick way to fix a credit score.

Improving FICO Scores

Beware of any advice that claims to improve your credit score fast. Sign up for credit-monitoring services to alert you instantly when there are changes to credit file

There are many credit reporting agencies, or credit bureaus, in the United States, but most people are familiar with the big three: Equifax, Experian, and TransUnion.

Credit score repair begins with your credit report. If you haven't done so, request one now! Your credit report contains the data used to calculate your credit score, and it may contain errors, so it's imperative to find and dispute inaccurate information. Focus on your late payments. Are they reported correctly? Other things to check are amounts owed. If you find errors on any of your reports, dispute them with the credit bureau.

Pull your credit now.

Equifax—www.equifax.com
P. O. Box 740241
Atlanta, Georgia 30374-0241
1-800-685-1111

Experian—www.experian.com
P. O. Box 2104
Allen, Texas 75013-0949
1-888-EXPERIAN (397-3742)

TransUnion—www.transunion.com
P. O. Box 1000
Chester, Pennsylvania 19022
1-800-916-8800

Follow the tips below today to improve your score:

Setup Payment Reminders

Making your credit payments on time is one of the biggest contributing factors to your credit scores. Take advantage of payment reminders that send you emails or texts when payments are due. Enroll in automatic payments through your credit card and loan providers to have payments automatically debited from your bank account.

Reduce Debt

This is easier said than done, but reducing the amount that you owe is going to be a far more satisfying achievement than improving your credit score. Stop using your credit cards. Use your credit report to make a list of all of your accounts and then go online or check recent statements to determine how much you owe on each account and what interest rate they are charging you. Come up with a payment plan that puts most of your available budget for debt payments toward the highest interest cards first, while maintaining minimum payments on your other accounts.

Pay Bills on Time

If you are having trouble making ends meet, contact your creditors or see a legitimate credit counselor. Your payment history contributes to 35 percent of your FICO score. There is no easy fix to missed or late payments, and delinquent payments have a major impact on your score. Pay your bills on time after being late, and your score should increase. The impact of past credit problems on your FICO scores fades as time passes.

Other Helpful Credit Information

- Paying off a collection account will not remove it from your credit report, and it will stay on your report for seven years.
- Reach out to a credit counselor if you're having difficulty making ends meet.
- Amounts are key in credit management—this category contributes 30 percent to your FICO score's calculation. Also, it's often easier to clean up than payment history. With discipline and the following information, you will see improvements in your score:

o   Keep balances low on credit cards and other "revolving credit."
o   Pay off debt rather than moving it around.
o   Don't close unused credit cards.
o   Don't open a number of new credit cards that you don't need.

To summarize if your goal is increasing your FICO score, it's about fixing the errors, being patient, taking measure prevent identify theft. When you have good credit, you have countless options to fund your deal.

CHAPTER 4

Using Your Home to Start Investing

Don't wait to buy real estate, buy real estate and wait.

—Will Rodgers

What Is a Home Equity Line of Credit (HELOC)?

A HELOC is a line of credit secured by your home that gives you a revolving credit that can finance your deal. With a HELOC, you're borrowing against the available equity in your home, and the house is used as collateral for the line of credit. Typically, you can borrow up to 85 percent of the value of your home, minus what you owe.

Similar to a credit card, as you repay your outstanding balance, the amount of available credit is replenished. You can borrow as little or as much as you need throughout your draw period, usually ten years, up to the established credit limit. Contact your locating banking institutions to learn more about their HELOC options.

Why Use HELOC to Buy Investment Properties?

Using a HELOC as down payment for investment property allows you to borrow money to make money. If the thought of debt binds you from taking action, get over it, or you won't be a successful real estate investor.

If the cost of borrowing is less than the income it produces, you're winning!

Let's Do the Math to See the Value in a HELOC

With a 4 percent interest on your HELOC, for example, $100,000 will cost you approximately $33.33 over the month. If you only acquire cash-flowing properties, this cost of the interest-only HELOC is covered, and you have extra income left over. Also, the interest cost is tax deductible because the funds are borrowed for investment purposes: bonus!

How do you obtain a HELOC?

Many lending institutions provide HELOC loans, like Quicken Loans, Chase, Discover, credit unions, and others. These loans can be used to make the needed improvements and purchase appliances for your flip.

CHAPTER 5

Using Credit and Not Cash to Purchase Investment Property Case Study

Money is a poor man's credit card.

—Marshall McLuhan

During the economic downturn, properties could be purchased at highway robbery prices. Most of us didn't take advantage of those opportunities because we didn't know if the recession would persist for decades. When I noticed condos at the prestigious Twelve Hotel in Atlanta were selling for $90K (three years earlier they were selling for $250K and up), I knew it would be a great investment opportunity for my dad and mom.

He financed with a HELOC that he took out against a property that he owned free and clear. Now my parents' condo is worth $300K. As a part-time real estate investor, my dad continued to buy several more properties without using cash.

My dad's story is an example of how the working man and woman who earns less than six figures on the job can use his or her credit to build wealth in real estate. Additionally, anyone can use creative financing to accomplish their end goal.

Seasoned investors use HELOCs and credit cards as a practical source of funding for them, not because they have no other options. These methods for buying property can be a cheaper way to finance your deal because you don't have to start paying interest until the bill is due. That gives you a few weeks to float purchases for free.

CHAPTER 6

How to Get Property with No Money and No Credit

I am so broke. A thief broke into my house last night. He started searching for money, so I woke up and started to search with him.

—Anonymous

We had you complete the financial statement, and you just learned that you are worth $500. As you face reality, you feel stuck. You focused on how much money you have. It doesn't take money to make money; it takes guts and courage. Chase is the deal, not your budget. In other words, buy the house at 65 cents on the dollar or lower and make the renovations that are needed for the home to sell at full asking price. Don't rehab based on what's in your budget. If it takes X dollars to make a kitchen sell for full asking, then you spend the money and don't make excuses about what you budgeted.

You can make money in a real estate transaction without anything coming from your pocket.

It's not easy, but we have some helpful tips on how to use other people's money to fund your deal.

There's a lot of people out there right now who have money sitting in the bank. You have friends, coworkers and relatives giving their money to people on Wall Street they don't know. They have cash in mutual funds, self-directed IRAs, and 401(k)s that are not giving them the type of return on investment (ROI) that you will offer. Convince friends, family, colleagues, or friends of friends to go in with you. Other sources to fund your deals are private money lenders, joint ventures, self-directed, and other investment account and crown funding/REIT.

Friends, Family, Colleagues & Friends of Friends

Many real estate investors turn to friends and family for their first funding needs. It is easy to make a sales pitch to people you're comfortable around and who are likely to say yes. Make an impression by putting together a presentation or package that contains details about the property, expected cost, project completion date, and estimated days on the market. It's important to communicate the terms and agreements to avoid conflict later with people you love. To keep that funding source available in the future, communicate often and pay your interest payments promptly to build confidence.

Action Step: Write down three friends and family members you can approach for funding who have at least $100,000 in their 401(k)s or self-directed IRAs, earning standard interest. You can entice them by securing their investment by promissory note and security deed at 70 percent of the after-repair value of the property.

TOP SECRET

**Friends and family only care about a sound plan that
is going to get their money back with interest!**

First, just because you need a loan doesn't mean you are a loser. The chances are good that many of the people you are about to approach were in your shoes at one time or another. Not only are they sympathetic and predisposed to help you out, but also they are not going to judge you. They know what it's like to be in your situation. You aren't the first person to ever hit up a friend for some dough, and you won't be the last. Keep your perspective.

People who make loans care about one thing—getting their money back as promised, with interest. Sure, your kin wants to help you. But if we're talking about anything more than ice-cream money, they want security and earnings for their stash.

**Money represents a real investing idea backed
by confidence and confidence.**

On the lines provided below, make a list of candidates who might be willing to invest in you. At the top of the list, jot down the names of people who are ablest to make the loan and who you believe have the willingness to do so.

Even if you are sure the person at the top of the list is going to write you a big, fat check, keep adding names to your list. You want to have a large list of potential backers because you never really know what someone is going to do until they do it. And you don't want to depend on any one person. If you have a long list of candidates, you'll be able to approach each person with a more positive and encouraging attitude because you won't come off as being desperate.

Represent your real estate investing plan well. Be knowledgeable, confident, and trustworthy to earn your potential investor's respect.

Before you speak anyone, work out exactly how you're going to repay them with interest and when you're going to do it. Make sure you can afford the payments and show them how. To create a circle of trust, show them your income and expenses. Your potential investor will be impressed and more likely to invest in your investment idea if you have a detailed plan that you explain in detail to them, revealing your own finances.

Using Joint-Venture Agreements

During 2010 and 2011 when we were growing our portfolio from scratch, we were averaging two rehabbed homes almost every month, and the majority of our purchases were joint ventures.

The majority of these deals were structured so that we were the managing partners (finding the deals, negotiating them, hiring the teams, and overseeing the renovations and management), and our money partners came to the table with financing capability and the initial investment capital required—down payment and closing costs.

We used joint ventures to build our cash reserves after we lost all of our real estate portfolio, except our personal home, filed for bankruptcy, and lost our creditworthiness during the real estate collapse.

How We Structure Joint-Venture Real Estate Deals

There isn't one right way to structure a JV. Your position in the JV will be based on your real estate investing career. If you are a novice real estate investor, you will discover the way that is the fairest for you and your partners. It depends on what you bring to the table.

Our partners put in 100 percent of the initial investment capital (e.g., down payment and closing costs). When we sell the property, their initial investment is repaid first, then any capital we have invested, and then we split the proceeds as per the agreement.

Our partners typically receive 49–60 percent annually ROI without putting forward any effort in the renovation process. Our partners know that they can't see those types of return from most investment tools.

Our JV partners typically own successful businesses, are in thriving careers, or are retired. They want to be in real estate, but they don't have the time or inclination to become experts. Our partners benefit from our $500,000 in real-estate-investing and business-transformation education and the years we've put into learning what to do to minimize risks and maximize returns and our proven history of success.

Today, we don't use joint ventures very often because it's lots of work to give up fifty/fifty on a long-term basis. Now we only have joint-venture partnerships with our regular investors. To reduce stress, be sure to document roles, activities, deliverables, cost, and risk, and communicate frequently in your JV partnership.

To attract our JV partners, we use the following simple flyer to covey the benefits of our partner relationship.

Ready to start making your money work for you?
Ear on your self-directed IRA, 401, CDs, or saving

Six Benefits to Becoming a Private Mortgage Lender

Your Investment Is Protected
Secured by a security deed and promissory note and listed as loss payee on the hazard insurance policy.

You Have Excellent Collateral

Loans are based on 70% loan to value (LTV) on local real estate.

You Do Not Have to Collect

The payments are forwarded directly to your account monthly.

You Have No Costs

Borrower pays all of the costs.

Your Earnings Are Tax Deferred

You still have advantage of the deferred tax using your self- directed IRA or other pension plan.

You Do Not Need a Lot of Money

Your available capital is tailored to the borrower's needs ($84,000-$98,000 Avg. Loan)

A Case Study for Joint Ventures

Below are actual examples of one of our joint-venture agreements and the supporting documents, promissory note, and security deed that protect you and your JV partner. You can take the template to your attorney for review. Additionally, study the documentation thoroughly for understanding. Don't fake it until you make it. Be confident through study and implementation. Learn and do!.

Joint Venture Agreement

This Joint Venture Agreement (the "Agreement") is made and entered into this 20th day of January 2017, by and between **BEST BUY HOMES, LLC,** a limited liability company organized and existing under the laws of the State of Georgia (referred to herein as "BBH") and **CKB HOMES, INC.** an individual resident of the 2655 Bethany Creek Ct.; Milton, Ga. 30034 (referred to herein as "CKB").

WHEREAS the parties desire to conduct the business of purchasing, renovating and selling the single family home located at **1078 ASHBY**

STREET SW; ATLANTA GEORGIA 30314 (referred to herein as the "Property") together; and

WHEREAS, CKB is willing to finance the operation of the business and BBH is willing to manage the business including the purchase, renovation, marketing and sale of the Property;

NOW, THEREFORE, in consideration of the covenants, representations, conditions and agreements set forth herein and for other good and valuable consideration, the receipt and sufficiency of which are hereby acknowledged, the parties hereto agree as follows:

1. **Scope and Description.** By this Agreement, the parties hereby create a for-profit joint venture for the purposes described in the preamble above (herein referred to as the "Business"). The joint venture shall be conducted under the name of "*1078 ASHBY STREET*" whose business address shall be 825 Golf View Ct., Dacula, Ga. 30019.

2. **Contributions.** **CKB** shall contribute the amount of **One Hundred Nineteen Thousand Dollars ($119,000.00)** to the joint venture. **BBH** shall contribute the Property and its time, skill and construction and marketing expertise for the duration of the joint venture, to ensure its success. Contributions shall be made on or before **January 20, 2017.**

Failure to complete the contribution on or before said date shall result in an immediate termination of this Agreement.

3. **Conduct of Venture.** BB shall be responsible for management of the joint venture and the Business and shall devote such time to its management is it deems necessary to ensure its success. BB shall have the authority, without the need to consult GG to: (a) execute all documents necessary or desirable to purchase the Property, (b) purchase materials and hire contractors, subcontractors and other workers or trades, (c) manage the construction of the renovation of the Property, (d) market the Property for Sale, (e) make draws

from the construction escrow account as needed to complete the renovation of the Property, (f) manage the finances of the business including opening such accounts as may be necessary or desirable, to accept and pay money on behalf of the Business and to keep all books and records of the Business (g) execute all documents necessary or desirable to sell the Property. Such authority may be increased or decreased from time to time upon mutual agreement of the parties. Renovation overruns are inevitable and will be funded by BBH if such occurs. BBH agrees to fund all expenses past $119,000 and get reimbursed at sale of property.

4. **Title to Property.** Legal title to all property acquired by the joint venture, whether real or personal, shall be taken in the name of Best Buy Homes, LLC., as trustee for the parties, and shall be held for their interest. The interest of each party in such property shall be proportionate to his or her share of the profits of the joint venture. Upon taking of title to the Property, Best Buy Homes, LLC shall execute a **Promissory Note in the amount of $119,000.00 in favor of ABC, LLC and shall execute a Deed to Secure Debt conveying title to the Property as security for said Promissory Note. ABC, LLC IS GUARANTEED PRINCIPAL AND 10% INTEREST.**

5. **Division of Profits.** The net profits earned by the joint venture shall be calculated upon the sale of the Property and shall be divided among the parties as follows: **BBH shall receive fifty percent (50%) and CKB shall receive fifty percent (50%).** No other remuneration shall be received by the parties from the joint venture. The net profits shall be calculated by first deducting all operating expenses from the gross income of the joint venture.

Estimate Profit
$170,000 Sales price X 70% = $119,000 (might list between $180-200,000)
-119,000 Investment
-10,200 6% Real Estate commissions
-5,100 3% Buyers Closing Costs
-1,000 home warranty, misc,
-1,000 Selling agent bonus
$33,700 / 2 = $16,850/$119,000 =.20.1 % R.O.I in 4 months X 3 = 63%
% Annual R.O.I

***Considering listing at$180,000

6. **Apportionment of Losses.** The parties shall bear any net loss sustained by the venture in any fiscal year as follows: **BB shall bear Fifty percent (50 %) of such loss, and CP shall bear fifty percent (50 %).** Any assessment against a party for a loss shall be payable to the joint venture not later than 30 days after the close of each calendar year.

7. **Records and Accounting.** BB shall maintain or cause to be maintained a complete set of records, statements, and accounts concerning the total operation of the joint venture, in which books shall be entered, fully and accurately, each transaction pertaining to the Business. All books will be open at all times for inspection and examination by CP or his agents. The fiscal year of the joint venture shall be the calendar year.

8. **Insurance and Surety Bonds.** The joint venture shall obtain insurance to cover the following items and types of losses. Builders Risk Policy. The premiums for such coverages shall be recognized as business expenses of the joint venture.

9. **Assignments and Transfers.** Neither party shall assign or transfer his or her rights or duties in the joint venture without the express written consent of the other party. Any purported transfer or assignment made without the consent of the other party shall be null and void and shall not relieve the transferor or assignor of his or her duties or obligations under this Agreement.

10. **Arbitration.** The assignment of specific duties and authority to BB hereunder was made to avoid major differences between the parties as to the conduct of the joint venture. The parties declare that the terms of this Agreement are controlling as to each of them. In the event of any disagreement between the parties with respect to any matter, the questions and disagreement shall be submitted for binding arbitration in Gwinnett County, Georgia and pursuant to the Commercial Arbitration Rules of the American Arbitration Association ("AAA"), with the sole arbitrator being selected by the parties pursuant to the above-referenced AAA rules. The expenses of arbitration shall be borne by the losing party or be apportioned between the parties as the arbitrator may direct, and judgment upon any arbitration award rendered by the arbitrator may be entered in any court of competent jurisdiction.

11. **Death or Dissolution**. The death or dissolution of a party shall cause the joint venture to be dissolved as soon as practical after such event and all net profits and proceeds from the sale of the assets of the joint venture shall be divided between the surviving party and the legal representative the deceased or dissolved party.

12. **Termination of Agreement**. Upon termination of this Agreement for any cause whatever, the joint venture shall be wound up and dissolved in accordance with the laws of the State of Georgia.

13. **Miscellaneous.**

    (a) This Agreement constitutes the entire agreement between the parties with respect to the transactions contemplated hereby, supersede any and all prior discussions and agreements and all such agreements are hereby terminated;
    (b) This Agreement shall be binding upon, inure to the benefit of, and be enforceable by the parties hereto and their legal representatives, successors and assigns;
    (c) This Agreement shall not confer any right or remedies upon any individual other than the parties hereto and their respective successors and permitted assigns;

(d) This Agreement may not be waived, modified, altered or amended in any manner except with the written consent of both parties;

(e) This Agreement may be executed simultaneously in one or more counterparts, each one of which shall be deemed an original, but all of which together shall constitute one and the same instrument;

(f) This Agreement shall be construed and interpreted by and governed in accordance with the laws of the State of Georgia. The parties hereby consent to personal jurisdiction over matters relating to this Agreement and interpretation thereof and to venue in the Courts of the State of Georgia;

(g) The parties hereto as individuals, principals, officers, partners and employees and on behalf of their heirs, administrators, executors or successors, agree to take all actions and to execute and deliver any and all documents reasonably necessary to effectuate all of the provisions of this Agreement.

(h) If any provision, clause or part hereof or the application thereof under certain circumstances is held invalid, illegal or unenforceable in any respect, the validity and enforceability of the remaining provisions hereof, or the application of any such provision, clause or part under other circumstances, shall not be in any way affected or impaired thereby. To the extent such determination is likely to give rise to a material adverse effect, the parties shall endeavor in good faith to replace the invalid, illegal or unenforceable provisions with valid provisions the economic effect of which comes as close as practical to that of the invalid, illegal or unenforceable provision.

Executed this 20 day of January, 2017.

Partner Company, Inc.

By: _____**(Seal)**

ABC, INC-President

Best Buy Homes, LLC

By: _____

Michael S. Cherwenka-Member
Signed, sealed and delivered
This 20st day of January, 2017,
in the presence of:

_____

Witness
_____NOTARY PUBLIC (Notary Seal)

Below is an example of a security deed that you can use.

[Space Above This Line for Recording Data]
Security Deed

DEFINITIONS

Words used in multiple sections of this document are defined below and other words are defined in Sections 3, 11, 13, 18, 20 and 21. Certain rules regarding the usage of words used in this document are also provided in Section 16.

(A) "Security Instrument" means this document, which is dated **January 20, 2017**, together with all Riders to this document.

(B) "Borrower" is **Best Buy Homes, LLC**. Borrower is the grantor under this Security Instrument.

(C) "Lender" is **CKB HOMES, INC.** Lender's address is 2655 Bethany Creek Ct.; Milton, Ga. 30034. Lender is the grantee under this Security Instrument.

(D) "Note" means the promissory note signed by Borrower and dated January 20, 2017. The Note states that Borrower owes Lender **One Hundred Nineteen Thousand Dollars and 00/100 (U.S. $119,000.00)**. Borrower has promised to pay this debt in regular Periodic Payments and to pay the debt in full not later than January 20, 2018.

(E) "Property" means the property that is described below under the heading "Transfer of Rights in the Property."

(F) "Loan" means the debt evidenced by the Note, plus interest, any prepayment charges and late charges due under the Note, and all sums due under this Security Instrument, plus interest.

(G) "Riders" means all Riders to this Security Instrument that are executed by Borrower. The following Riders are to be executed by Borrower [check box as applicable]:

- o   Adjustable Rate Rider □ Condominium Rider
- o   Second Home Rider
- o   Balloon Rider □ Planned Unit Development Rider
- o   Other(s) [specify] _____
- o   1-4 Family Rider □ Biweekly Payment Rider

(H) "Applicable Law" means all controlling applicable federal, state and local statutes, regulations, ordinances and administrative rules and orders (that have the effect of law) as well as all applicable final, non-appealable judicial opinions.

(I) "Community Association Dues, Fees, and Assessments" means all dues, fees, assessments and other charges that are imposed on Borrower or the Property by a condominium association, homeowner's association or similar organization.

(J) "Electronic Funds Transfer" means any transfer of funds, other than a transaction originated by check, draft, or similar paper instrument, which is initiated through an electronic terminal, telephonic instrument, computer, or magnetic tape so as to order, instruct, or authorize a financial institution to debit or credit an account. Such term includes, but is not limited to, point-of-sale transfers, automated teller machine transactions, transfers initiated by telephone, wire transfers, and automated clearinghouse transfers.

(K) "Escrow Items" means those items that are described in Section 3.

(L) "Miscellaneous Proceeds" means any compensation, settlement, award of damages, or proceeds paid by any third party (other than insurance proceeds paid under the coverages described in Section 5) for: (I) damage to, or destruction of, the Property; (ii) condemnation or other taking of all or any part of the Property; (iii) conveyance in lieu of condemnation;

or (iv) misrepresentations of, or omissions as to, the value and/or condition of the Property.

(M) "Mortgage Insurance" means insurance protecting Lender against the nonpayment of, or default on, the Loan.

(N) "Periodic Payment" means the regularly scheduled amount due for (I) principal and interest under the Note, plus (ii) any amounts under Section 3 of this Security Instrument.

(O) "RESPA" means the Real Estate Settlement Procedures Act (12 U.S.C. §2601 et seq.) and its implementing regulation, Regulation X (24 C.F.R. Part 3500), as they might be amended from time to time, or any additional or successor legislation or regulation that governs the same subject matter. As used in this Security Instrument, "RESPA" refers to all requirements and restrictions that are imposed in regard to a "federally related mortgage loan" even if the Loan does not qualify as a "federally related mortgage loan" under RESPA.

(P) "Successor in Interest of Borrower" means any party that has taken title to the Property, whether or not that party has assumed Borrower's obligations under the Note and/or this Security Instrument.

Transfer of Rights in the Property

This Security Instrument secures to Lender: (I) the repayment of the Loan, and all renewals, extensions and modifications of the Note; and (ii) the performance of Borrower's covenants and agreements under this Security Instrument and the Note. For this purpose, Borrower does hereby grant and convey to Lender and Lender's successors and assigns, with power of sale, the following described property located in the **County of Fulton.**

which currently has the address of **1078 ASHBY GROVE SW; ATLANTA, Ga. 30314** ("Property Address"):

TO HAVE AND TO HOLD this property unto Lender and Lender's successors and assigns, forever, together with all the improvements now or hereafter erected on the property, and all easements, appurtenances, and fixtures now or hereafter a part of the property. All replacements and additions shall also be covered by this Security Instrument. All of the foregoing is referred to in this Security Instrument as the "Property."

BORROWER COVENANTS that Borrower is lawfully seized of the estate hereby conveyed and has the right to grant and convey the Property and that the Property is unencumbered, except for encumbrances of record. Borrower warrants and will defend generally the title to the Property against all claims and demands, subject to any encumbrances of record.

THIS SECURITY INSTRUMENT combines uniform covenants for national use and non-uniform covenants with limited variations by jurisdiction to constitute a uniform security instrument covering real property.

UNIFORM COVENANTS. Borrower and Lender covenant and agree as follows:

1. Payment of Principal, Interest, Escrow Items, Prepayment Charges, and Late Charges. Borrower shall pay when due the principal of, and interest on, the debt evidenced by the Note and any prepayment charges and late charges due under the Note. Borrower shall also pay funds for Escrow Items pursuant to Section 3. Payments due under the Note and this Security Instrument shall be made in U.S. currency. However, if any check or other instrument received by Lender as payment under the Note or this Security Instrument is returned to Lender unpaid, Lender may require that any or all subsequent payments due under the Note and this Security Instrument be made in one or more of the following forms, as selected by Lender: (a) cash; (b) money order; (c) certified check, bank check, treasurer's check or cashier's check, provided any such check is drawn upon an institution whose deposits are insured by a federal agency, instrumentality, or entity; or (d) Electronic Funds Transfer.

Payments are deemed received by Lender when received at the location designated in the Note or at such other location as may be designated by Lender in accordance with the notice provisions in Section 15. Lender may return any payment or partial payment if the payment or partial payments are insufficient to bring the Loan current. Lender may accept any payment or partial payment insufficient to bring the Loan current, without waiver of any rights hereunder or prejudice to its rights to refuse such payment or partial payments in the future, but Lender is not obligated to apply such payments at the time such payments are accepted. If each Periodic Payment is applied as of its scheduled due date, then Lender need not pay interest on unapplied funds. Lender may hold such unapplied funds until Borrower makes payment to bring the Loan current. If Borrower does not do so within a reasonable period of time, Lender shall either apply such funds or return them to Borrower. If not applied earlier, such funds will be applied to the outstanding principal balance under the Note immediately prior to foreclosure. No offset or claim which Borrower might have now or in the future against Lender shall relieve Borrower from making payments due under the Note and this Security Instrument or performing the covenants and agreements secured by this Security Instrument.

2. Application of Payments or Proceeds. Except as otherwise described in this Section 2, all payments accepted and applied by Lender shall be applied in the following order of priority: (a) interest due under the Note; (b) principal due under the Note; (c) amounts due under Section 3. Such payments shall be applied to each Periodic Payment in the order in which it became due. Any remaining amounts shall be applied first to late charges, second to any other amounts due under this Security Instrument, and then to reduce the principal balance of the Note.

If Lender receives a payment from Borrower for a delinquent Periodic Payment which includes a sufficient amount to pay any late charge due, the payment may be applied to the delinquent payment and the late charge. If more than one Periodic Payment is outstanding, Lender may apply any payment received from Borrower to the repayment of the Periodic Payments if, and to the extent that, each payment can be paid in full. To the extent that any excess exists after the payment is applied to the full payment of one or more Periodic Payments, such excess may be applied to any late charges due. Voluntary prepayments shall be applied first to any prepayment charges and then as described in the Note.

Any application of payments, insurance proceeds, or Miscellaneous Proceeds to principal due under the Note shall not extend or postpone the due date, or change the amount, of the Periodic Payments.

3. Funds for Escrow Items. Borrower shall pay to Lender on the day Periodic Payments are due under the Note, until the Note is paid in full, a sum (the "Funds") to provide for payment of amounts due for: (a) taxes and assessments and other items which can attain priority over this Security Instrument as a lien or encumbrance on the Property; (b) leasehold payments or ground rents on the Property, if any; (c) premiums for any and all insurance required by Lender under Section 5; and (d) Mortgage Insurance premiums, if any, or any sums payable by Borrower to Lender in lieu of the payment of Mortgage Insurance premiums in accordance with the provisions of Section 10. These items are called "Escrow Items." At origination or at any time during the term of the Loan, Lender may require that Community Association Dues, Fees, and Assessments, if any, be escrowed by Borrower, and such dues, fees and assessments shall be an Escrow Item. Borrower shall promptly furnish to Lender all notices of amounts to be paid under this Section. Borrower shall pay Lender the Funds for Escrow Items unless Lender waives Borrower's obligation to pay the Funds for any or all Escrow Items. Lender may waive Borrower's obligation to pay to Lender Funds for any or all Escrow Items at any time. Any such waiver may only be in writing. In the event of such waiver, Borrower shall pay directly, when and where payable, the amounts due for any Escrow Items for which payment of Funds has been waived by Lender and, if Lender requires, shall furnish to Lender receipts evidencing such payment within such time period as Lender may require. Borrower's obligation to make such payments and to provide receipts shall for all purposes be deemed to be a covenant and agreement contained in this Security Instrument, as the phrase "covenant and agreement" is used in Section 9. If Borrower is obligated to pay Escrow Items directly, pursuant to a waiver, and Borrower fails to pay the amount due for an Escrow Item, Lender may exercise its rights under Section 9 and pay such amount and Borrower shall then be obligated under Section 9 to repay to Lender any such amount. Lender may revoke the waiver as to any or all Escrow Items at any time by a notice given in accordance with Section 15 and, upon such revocation, Borrower shall pay to Lender all Funds, and in such amounts, that are then required under this Section 3.

Lender may, at any time, collect and hold Funds in an amount (a) sufficient to permit Lender to apply the Funds at the time specified under RESPA, and (b) not to exceed the maximum amount a lender can require under RESPA. Lender shall estimate the amount of Funds due on the basis of current data and reasonable estimates of expenditures of future Escrow Items or otherwise in accordance with Applicable Law.

The Funds shall be held in an institution whose deposits are insured by a federal agency, instrumentality, or entity (including Lender, if Lender is an institution whose deposits are so insured) or in any Federal Home Loan Bank. Lender shall apply the Funds to pay the Escrow Items no later than the time specified under RESPA. Lender shall not charge Borrower for holding and applying the Funds, annually analyzing the escrow account, or verifying the Escrow Items, unless Lender pays Borrower interest on the Funds and Applicable Law Permits Lender to make such a charge. Unless an agreement is made in writing or Applicable Law requires interest to be paid on the Funds, Lender shall not be required to pay Borrower any interest or earnings on the Funds. Borrower and Lender can agree in writing, however, that interest shall be paid on the Funds. Lender shall give to Borrower, without charge, an annual accounting of the Funds as required by RESPA.

If there is a surplus of Funds held in escrow, as defined under RESPA, Lender shall account to Borrower for the excess funds in accordance with RESPA. If there is a shortage of Funds held in escrow, as defined under RESPA, Lender shall notify Borrower as required by RESPA, and Borrower shall pay to Lender the amount necessary to make up the shortage in accordance with RESPA, but in no more than 12 monthly payments. If there is a deficiency of Funds held in escrow, as defined under RESPA, Lender shall notify Borrower as required by RESPA, and Borrower shall pay to Lender the amount necessary to make up the deficiency in accordance with RESPA, but in no more than 12 monthly payments.

Upon payment in full of all sums secured by this Security Instrument, Lender shall promptly refund to Borrower any Funds held by Lender.

4. Charges; Liens. Borrower shall pay all taxes, assessments, charges, fines, and impositions attributable to the Property which can attain priority over this Security Instrument, leasehold payments or ground rents on the Property, if any, and Community Association Dues, Fees, and Assessments, if any. To the extent that these items are Escrow Items, Borrower shall pay them in the manner provided in Section 3.

Borrower shall promptly discharge any lien which has priority over this Security Instrument unless Borrower: (a) agrees in writing to the payment of the obligation secured by the lien in a manner acceptable to Lender, but only so long as Borrower is performing such agreement; (b) contests the lien in good faith by, or defends against enforcement of the lien in, legal proceedings which in Lender's opinion operate to prevent the enforcement of the lien while those proceedings are pending, but only until such proceedings are concluded; or (c) secures from the holder of the lien an agreement satisfactory to Lender subordinating the lien to this Security Instrument. If Lender determines that any part of the Property is subject to a lien which can attain priority over this Security Instrument, Lender may give Borrower a notice identifying the lien. Within 10 days of the date on which that notice is given, Borrower shall satisfy the lien or take one or more of the actions set forth above in this Section 4.

Lender may require Borrower to pay a one-time charge for a real estate tax verification and/or reporting service used by Lender in connection with this Loan.

5. Property Insurance. Borrower shall keep the improvements now existing or hereafter erected on the Property insured against loss by fire, hazards included within the term "extended coverage," and any other hazards including, but not limited to, earthquakes and floods, for which Lender requires insurance. This insurance shall be maintained in the amounts (including deductible levels) and for the periods that Lender requires. What Lender requires pursuant to the preceding sentences can change during the term of the Loan. The insurance carrier providing the insurance shall be chosen by Borrower subject to Lender's right to disapprove Borrower's choice, which right shall not be exercised unreasonably. Lender may require Borrower to pay, in connection with this Loan, either: (a) a one-time charge for flood zone determination, certification and tracking services; or (b) a one-time charge for flood zone determination and certification services and subsequent charges each time remapping's or similar changes occur which reasonably might affect such determination or certification. Borrower shall also be responsible for the payment of any fees imposed by the Federal Emergency Management Agency in connection with the review of any flood zone determination resulting from an objection by Borrower.

If Borrower fails to maintain any of the coverages described above, Lender may obtain insurance coverage, at Lender's option and Borrower's expense. Lender is under no obligation to purchase any particular type or amount of coverage. Therefore, such coverage shall cover Lender, but might or might not protect Borrower, Borrower's equity in the Property, or the contents of the Property, against any risk, hazard or liability and might provide greater or lesser coverage than was previously in effect. Borrower acknowledges that the cost of the insurance coverage so obtained might significantly exceed the cost of insurance that Borrower could have obtained. Any amounts disbursed by Lender under this Section 5 shall become additional debt of Borrower secured by this Security Instrument. These amounts shall bear interest at the Note rate from the date of disbursement and shall be payable, with such interest, upon notice from Lender to Borrower requesting payment.

All insurance policies required by Lender and renewals of such policies shall be subject to Lender's right to disapprove such policies, shall include a standard mortgage clause, and shall name Lender as mortgagee and/or as an additional loss payee. Lender shall have the right to hold the policies and renewal certificates. If Lender requires, Borrower shall promptly give to Lender all receipts of paid premiums and renewal notices. If Borrower obtains any form of insurance coverage, not otherwise required by Lender, for damage to, or destruction of, the Property, such policy shall include a standard mortgage clause and shall name Lender as mortgagee and/or as an additional loss payee.

In the event of loss, Borrower shall give prompt notice to the insurance carrier and Lender. Lender may make proof of loss if not made promptly by Borrower. Unless Lender and Borrower otherwise agree in writing, any insurance proceeds, whether or not the underlying insurance was required by Lender, shall be applied to restoration or repair of the Property, if the restoration or repair is economically feasible and Lender's security is not lessened. During such repair and restoration period, Lender shall have the right to hold such insurance proceeds until Lender has had an opportunity to inspect such Property to ensure the work has been completed to Lender's satisfaction, provided that such inspection shall be undertaken promptly. Lender may disburse proceeds for the repairs and restoration in a single payment or in a series of progress payments as the work is completed. Unless an agreement is made in writing or Applicable Law requires interest to be paid on such insurance proceeds, Lender shall not be required to pay Borrower any interest or earnings on such proceeds. Fees for public adjusters, or other third parties, retained by Borrower shall not be paid out of the insurance proceeds and shall be the sole obligation of Borrower. If the restoration or repair is not economically feasible or Lender's security would be lessened, the insurance proceeds shall be applied to the sums secured by this Security Instrument, whether or not then due, with the excess, if any, paid to Borrower. Such insurance proceeds shall be applied in the order provided for in Section 2.

If Borrower abandons the Property, Lender may file, negotiate and settle any available insurance claim and related matters. If Borrower does not respond within 30 days to a notice from Lender that the insurance carrier has offered to settle a claim, then Lender may negotiate and settle the claim. The 30-day period will begin when the notice is given. In either event, or if Lender acquires the Property under Section 22 or otherwise, Borrower hereby assigns to Lender (a) Borrower's rights to any insurance proceeds in an amount not to exceed the amounts unpaid under the Note or this Security Instrument, and (b) any other of Borrower's rights (other than the right to any refund of unearned premiums paid by Borrower) under all insurance policies covering the Property, insofar as such rights are applicable to the coverage of the Property. Lender may use the insurance proceeds either to repair or restore the Property or to pay amounts unpaid under the Note or this Security Instrument, whether or not then due.

6. Occupancy. Borrower shall occupy, establish, and use the Property as Borrower's principal residence within 60 days after the execution of this Security Instrument and shall continue to occupy the Property as Borrower's principal residence for at least one year after the date of occupancy, unless Lender otherwise agrees in writing, which consent shall not be unreasonably withheld, or unless extenuating circumstances exist which are beyond Borrower's control.

7. Preservation, Maintenance and Protection of the Property; Inspections. Borrower shall not destroy, damage or impair the Property, allow the Property to deteriorate or commit waste on the Property. Whether or not Borrower is residing in the Property, Borrower shall maintain the Property in order to prevent the Property from deteriorating or decreasing in value due to its condition. Unless it is determined pursuant to Section 5 that repair or restoration is not economically feasible, Borrower shall promptly repair the Property if damaged to avoid further deterioration or damage. If insurance or condemnation proceeds are paid in connection with damage to, or the taking of, the Property, Borrower shall be responsible for repairing or restoring the Property only if Lender has released proceeds for such purposes. Lender may disburse proceeds for the repairs and restoration in a single payment or in a series of progress payments as the work is completed. If the insurance or condemnation proceeds are not sufficient to repair or restore the Property, Borrower is not relieved of Borrower's obligation for the completion of such repair or restoration.

Lender or its agent may make reasonable entries upon and inspections of the Property. If it has reasonable cause, Lender may inspect the interior of the improvements on the Property. Lender shall give Borrower notice at the time of or prior to such an interior inspection specifying such reasonable cause.

8. Borrower's Loan Application. Borrower shall be in default if, during the Loan application process, Borrower or any persons or entities acting at the direction of Borrower or with Borrower's knowledge or consent gave materially false, misleading, or inaccurate information or statements to Lender (or failed to provide Lender with material information) in connection with the Loan. Material representations include, but are not limited to, representations concerning Borrower's occupancy of the Property as Borrower's principal residence.

9. Protection of Lender's Interest in the Property and Rights Under this Security Instrument. If (a) Borrower fails to perform the covenants and agreements contained in this Security Instrument, (b) there is a legal proceeding that might significantly affect Lender's interest in the Property and/or rights under this Security Instrument (such as a proceeding in bankruptcy, probate, for condemnation or forfeiture, for enforcement of a lien which may attain priority over this Security Instrument or to enforce laws or regulations), or (c) Borrower has abandoned the Property, then Lender may do and pay for whatever is reasonable or appropriate to protect Lender's interest in the Property and rights under this Security Instrument, including protecting and/or assessing the value of the Property, and securing and/or repairing the Property (as set forth below). Lender's actions can include, but are not limited to: (a) paying any sums secured by a lien which has priority over this Security Instrument; (b) appearing in court; and (c) paying reasonable attorneys' fees to protect its interest in the Property and/or rights under this Security Instrument, including its secured position in a bankruptcy proceeding. Securing the Property includes, but is not limited to, making repairs, replacing doors and windows, draining water from pipes, and eliminating building or other code violations or dangerous conditions. Although Lender may take action under this Section 9, Lender does not have to do so and is not under any duty or obligation to do so. It is agreed that Lender incurs no liability for not taking any or all actions authorized under this Section 9.

Any amounts disbursed by Lender under this Section 9 shall become additional debt of Borrower secured by this Security Instrument. These amounts shall bear interest at the Note rate from the date of disbursement and shall be payable, with such interest, upon notice from Lender to Borrower requesting payment.

If this Security Instrument is on a leasehold, Borrower shall comply with all the provisions of the lease. If Borrower acquires fee title to the Property, the leasehold and the fee title shall not merge unless Lender agrees to the merger in writing.

10. Mortgage Insurance. If Lender required Mortgage Insurance as a condition of making the Loan, Borrower shall pay the premiums required to maintain the Mortgage Insurance in effect. If, for any reason, the Mortgage Insurance coverage required by Lender ceases to be available from the mortgage insurer that previously provided such insurance and Borrower was required to make separately designated payments toward the premiums for Mortgage Insurance, Borrower shall pay the premiums required to obtain coverage substantially equivalent to the Mortgage Insurance previously in effect, at a cost substantially equivalent to the cost to Borrower of the Mortgage Insurance previously in effect, from an alternate mortgage insurer selected by Lender. If substantially equivalent Mortgage Insurance coverage is not available, Borrower shall continue to pay to Lender the amount of the separately designated payments that were due when the insurance coverage ceased to be in effect. Lender will accept, use and retain these payments as a non-refundable loss reserve in lieu of Mortgage Insurance. Such loss reserve shall be non-refundable, notwithstanding the fact that the Loan is ultimately paid in full, and Lender shall not be required to pay Borrower any interest or earnings on such loss reserve. Lender can no longer require loss reserve payments if Mortgage Insurance coverage (in the amount and for the period that Lender requires) provided by an insurer selected by Lender again becomes available, is obtained, and Lender requires separately designated payments toward the premiums for Mortgage Insurance. If Lender required Mortgage Insurance as a condition of making the Loan and Borrower was required to make separately designated payments toward the premiums for Mortgage Insurance, Borrower shall pay the premiums required to maintain Mortgage Insurance in effect, or to provide a non-refundable loss reserve, until Lender's requirement for Mortgage Insurance ends in accordance with any written agreement between Borrower and Lender providing for such termination or until termination is required by Applicable Law. Nothing in this Section 10 affects Borrower's obligation to pay interest at the rate provided in the Note.

Mortgage Insurance reimburses Lender (or any entity that purchases the Note) for certain losses it may incur if Borrower does not repay the Loan as agreed. Borrower is not a party to the Mortgage Insurance.

Mortgage insurers evaluate their total risk on all such insurance in force from time to time, and may enter into agreements with other parties that share or modify their risk, or reduce losses. These agreements are on terms and conditions that are satisfactory to the mortgage insurer and the other party (or parties) to these agreements. These agreements may require the mortgage insurer to make payments using any source of funds that the mortgage insurer may have available (which may include funds obtained from Mortgage Insurance premiums).

As a result of these agreements, Lender, any purchaser of the Note, another insurer, any reinsurer, any other entity, or any affiliate of any of the foregoing, may receive (directly or indirectly) amounts that derive from (or might be characterized as) a portion of Borrower's payments for Mortgage Insurance, in exchange for sharing or modifying the mortgage insurer's risk, or reducing losses. If such agreement provides that an affiliate of Lender takes a share of the insurer's risk in exchange for a share of the premiums paid to the insurer, the arrangement is often termed "captive reinsurance." Further:

(a) Any such agreements will not affect the amounts that Borrower has agreed to pay for Mortgage Insurance, or any other terms of the Loan. Such agreements will not increase the amount Borrower will owe for Mortgage Insurance, and they will not entitle Borrower to any refund.

(b) Any such agreements will not affect the rights Borrower has - if any - with respect to the Mortgage Insurance under the Homeowners Protection Act of 1998 or any other law. These rights may include the right to receive certain disclosures, to request and obtain cancellation of the Mortgage Insurance, to have the Mortgage Insurance terminated automatically, and/or to receive a refund of any Mortgage Insurance premiums that were unearned at the time of such cancellation or termination.

11. Assignment of Miscellaneous Proceeds; Forfeiture. All Miscellaneous Proceeds are hereby assigned to and shall be paid to Lender.

If the Property is damaged, such Miscellaneous Proceeds shall be applied to restoration or repair of the Property, if the restoration or repair is economically feasible and Lender's security is not lessened. During such repair and restoration period, Lender shall have the right to hold such Miscellaneous Proceeds until Lender has had an opportunity to inspect such Property to ensure the work has been completed to Lender's satisfaction, provided that such inspection shall be undertaken promptly. Lender may pay for the repairs and restoration in a single disbursement or in a series of progress payments as the work is completed. Unless an agreement is made in writing or Applicable Law requires interest to be paid on such Miscellaneous Proceeds, Lender shall not be required to pay Borrower any interest or earnings on such Miscellaneous Proceeds. If the restoration or repair is not economically feasible or Lender's security would be lessened, the Miscellaneous Proceeds shall be applied to the sums secured by this Security Instrument, whether or not then due, with the excess, if any, paid to Borrower. Such Miscellaneous Proceeds shall be applied in the order provided for in Section 2.

In the event of a total taking, destruction, or loss in value of the Property, the Miscellaneous Proceeds shall be applied to the sums secured by this Security Instrument, whether or not then due, with the excess, if any, paid to Borrower.

In the event of a partial taking, destruction, or loss in value of the Property in which the fair market value of the Property immediately before the partial taking, destruction, or loss in value is equal to or greater than the amount of the sums secured by this Security Instrument immediately before the partial taking, destruction, or loss in value, unless Borrower and Lender otherwise agree in writing, the sums secured by this Security Instrument shall be reduced by the amount of the Miscellaneous Proceeds multiplied by the following fraction: (a) the total amount of the sums secured immediately before the partial taking, destruction, or loss in value divided by (b) the fair market value of the Property immediately before the partial taking, destruction, or loss in value. Any balance shall be paid to Borrower.

In the event of a partial taking, destruction, or loss in value of the Property in which the fair market value of the Property immediately before the partial taking, destruction, or loss in value is less than the amount of the sums secured immediately before the partial taking, destruction, or loss in value, unless Borrower and Lender otherwise agree in writing, the Miscellaneous Proceeds shall be applied to the sums secured by this Security Instrument whether or not the sums are then due.

If the Property is abandoned by Borrower, or if, after notice by Lender to Borrower that the Opposing Party (as defined in the next sentence) offers to make an award to settle a claim for damages, Borrower fails to respond to Lender within 30 days after the date the notice is given, Lender is authorized to collect and apply the Miscellaneous Proceeds either to restoration or repair of the Property or to the sums secured by this Security Instrument, whether or not then due. "Opposing Party" means the third party that owes Borrower Miscellaneous Proceeds or the party against whom Borrower has a right of action in regard to Miscellaneous Proceeds.

Borrower shall be in default if any action or proceeding, whether civil or criminal, is begun that, in Lender's judgment, could result in forfeiture of the Property or other material impairment of Lender's interest in the Property or rights under this Security Instrument. Borrower can cure such a default and, if acceleration has occurred, reinstate as provided in Section 19, by causing the action or proceeding to be dismissed with a ruling that, in Lender's judgment, precludes forfeiture of the Property or other material impairment of Lender's interest in the Property or rights under this Security Instrument. The proceeds of any award or claim for damages that are attributable to the impairment of Lender's interest in the Property are hereby assigned and shall be paid to Lender.

All Miscellaneous Proceeds that are not applied to restoration or repair of the Property shall be applied in the order provided for in Section 2.

12. Borrower Not Released; Forbearance by Lender Not a Waiver. Extension of the time for payment or modification of amortization of the sums secured by this Security Instrument granted by Lender to Borrower or any Successor in Interest of Borrower shall not operate to release the liability of Borrower or any Successors in Interest of Borrower. Lender shall not be required to commence proceedings against any Successor in Interest of Borrower or to refuse to extend time for payment or otherwise modify amortization of the sums secured by this Security Instrument by reason of any demand made by the original Borrower or any Successors in Interest of Borrower. Any forbearance by Lender in exercising any right or remedy including, without limitation, Lender's acceptance of payments from third persons, entities or Successors in Interest of Borrower or in amounts less than the amount then due, shall not be a waiver of or preclude the exercise of any right or remedy.

13. Joint and Several Liability; Co-signers; Successors and Assigns Bound. Borrower covenants and agrees that Borrower's obligations and liability shall be joint and several. However, any Borrower who co-signs this Security Instrument but does not execute the Note (a "co-signer"): (a) is co-signing this Security Instrument only to mortgage, grant and convey the co-signer's interest in the Property under the terms of this Security Instrument; (b) is not personally obligated to pay the sums secured by this Security Instrument; and (c) agrees that Lender and any other Borrower can agree to extend, modify, forbear or make any accommodations with regard to the terms of this Security Instrument or the Note without the co-signer's consent.

Subject to the provisions of Section 18, any Successor in Interest of Borrower who assumes Borrower's obligations under this Security

Instrument in writing, and is approved by Lender, shall obtain all of Borrower's rights and benefits under this Security Instrument. Borrower shall not be released from Borrower's obligations and liability under this Security Instrument unless Lender agrees to such release in writing. The covenants and agreements of this Security Instrument shall bind (except as provided in Section 20) and benefit the successors and assigns of Lender.

14. Loan Charges. Lender may charge Borrower fees for services performed in connection with Borrower's default, for the purpose of protecting Lender's interest in the Property and rights under this Security Instrument, including, but not limited to, attorneys' fees, property inspection and valuation fees. In regard to any other fees, the absence of express authority in this Security Instrument to charge a specific fee to Borrower shall not be construed as a prohibition on the charging of such fee. Lender may not charge fees that are expressly prohibited by this Security Instrument or by Applicable Law.

If the Loan is subject to a law which sets maximum loan charges, and that law is finally interpreted so that the interest or other loan charges collected or to be collected in connection with the Loan exceed the permitted limits, then: (a) any such loan charge shall be reduced by the amount necessary to reduce the charge to the permitted limit; and (b) any sums already collected from Borrower which exceeded permitted limits will be refunded to Borrower. Lender may choose to make this refund by reducing the principal owed under the Note or by making a direct payment to Borrower. If a refund reduces principal, the reduction will be treated as a partial prepayment without any prepayment charge (whether or not a prepayment charge is provided for under the Note). Borrower's acceptance of any such refund made by direct payment to Borrower will constitute a waiver of any right of action Borrower might have arising out of such overcharge.

15. Notices. All notices given by Borrower or Lender in connection with this Security Instrument must be in writing. Any notice to Borrower in connection with this Security Instrument shall be deemed to have been given to Borrower when mailed by first-class mail or when actually delivered to Borrower's notice address if sent by other means. Notice to any one Borrower shall constitute notice to all Borrowers unless Applicable Law expressly requires otherwise. The notice address shall be the Property Address unless Borrower has designated a substitute notice address by notice to Lender. Borrower shall promptly notify Lender of Borrower's change of address. If Lender specifies a procedure for reporting Borrower's change of address, then Borrower shall only report a change of address through that specified procedure. There may be only one designated notice address under this Security Instrument at any one time. Any notice to Lender shall be given by delivering it or by mailing it by first-class mail to Lender's address stated herein unless Lender has designated another address by notice to Borrower. Any notice in connection with this Security Instrument shall not be deemed to have been given to Lender until actually received by Lender. If any notice required by this Security Instrument is also required under Applicable Law, the Applicable Law requirement will satisfy the corresponding requirement under this Security Instrument.

16. Governing Law; Severability; Rules of Construction. This Security Instrument shall be governed by federal law and the law of the jurisdiction in which the Property is located. All rights and obligations contained in this Security Instrument are subject to any requirements and limitations of Applicable Law. Applicable Law might explicitly or implicitly allow the parties to agree by contract or it might be silent, but such silence shall not be construed as a prohibition against agreement by contract. In the event that any provision or clause of this Security Instrument or the Note conflicts with Applicable Law, such conflict shall not affect other provisions of this Security Instrument or the Note which can be given effect without the conflicting provision.

As used in this Security Instrument: (a) words of the masculine gender shall mean and include corresponding neuter words or words of the feminine gender; (b) words in the singular shall mean and include the plural and vice versa; and (c) the word "may" gives sole discretion without any obligation to take any action.

17. Borrower's Copy. Borrower shall be given one copy of the Note and of this Security Instrument.

18. Transfer of the Property or a Beneficial Interest in Borrower. As used in this Section 18, "Interest in the Property" means any legal or beneficial interest in the Property, including, but not limited to, those beneficial interests transferred in a bond for deed, contract for deed, installment sales contract or escrow agreement, the intent of which is the transfer of title by Borrower at a future date to a purchaser.

If all or any part of the Property or any Interest in the Property is sold or transferred (or if Borrower is not a natural person and a beneficial interest in Borrower is sold or transferred) without Lender's prior written consent, Lender may require immediate payment in full of all sums secured by this Security Instrument. However, this option shall not be exercised by Lender if such exercise is prohibited by Applicable Law.

If Lender exercises this option, Lender shall give Borrower notice of acceleration. The notice shall provide a period of not less than 30 days from the date the notice is given in accordance with Section 15 within which Borrower must pay all sums secured by this Security Instrument. If Borrower fails to pay these sums prior to the expiration of this period, Lender may invoke any remedies permitted by this Security Instrument without further notice or demand on Borrower.

19. Borrower's Right to Reinstate After Acceleration. If Borrower meets certain conditions, Borrower shall have the right to have enforcement of this Security Instrument discontinued at any time prior to the earliest of: (a) five days before sale of the Property pursuant to any power of sale contained in this Security Instrument; (b) such other period as Applicable Law might specify for the termination of Borrower's right to reinstate; or (c) entry of a judgment enforcing this Security Instrument. Those conditions are that Borrower: (a) pays Lender all sums which then would be due under this Security Instrument and the Note as if no acceleration had occurred; (b) cures any default of any other covenants or agreements; (c) pays all expenses incurred in enforcing this Security Instrument, including, but not limited to, reasonable attorneys' fees, property inspection and valuation fees, and other fees incurred for the purpose of protecting Lender's interest in the Property and rights under this Security Instrument; and (d) takes such action as Lender may reasonably require to assure that Lender's interest in the Property and rights under this Security Instrument, and Borrower's obligation to pay the sums secured by this Security Instrument, shall continue unchanged. Lender may require that Borrower pay such reinstatement sums and expenses in one or more of the following forms, as selected by Lender: (a) cash; (b) money order; (c) certified check, bank check, treasurer's check or cashier's check, provided any such check is drawn upon an institution whose deposits are insured by a federal agency, instrumentality or entity; or (d) Electronic Funds Transfer. Upon reinstatement by Borrower, this Security Instrument and obligations secured hereby shall remain fully effective as if no acceleration had occurred. However, this right to reinstate shall not apply in the case of acceleration under Section 18.

20. Sale of Note; Change of Loan Servicer; Notice of Grievance. The Note or a partial interest in the Note (together with this Security Instrument) can be sold one or more times without prior notice to Borrower. A sale might result in a change in the entity (known as the "Loan Servicer") that collects Periodic Payments due under the Note and this Security Instrument and performs other mortgage loan servicing obligations under the Note, this Security Instrument, and Applicable Law. There also might be one or more changes of the Loan Servicer unrelated to a sale of the Note. If there is a change of the Loan Servicer, Borrower will be given written notice of the change which will state the name and address of the new Loan Servicer, the address to which payments should be made and any other information RESPA requires in connection with a notice of transfer of servicing. If the Note is sold and thereafter the Loan is serviced by a Loan Servicer other than the purchaser of the Note, the mortgage loan servicing obligations to Borrower will remain with the Loan Servicer or be transferred to a successor Loan Servicer and are not assumed by the Note purchaser unless otherwise provided by the Note purchaser.

Neither Borrower nor Lender may commence, join, or be joined to any judicial action (as either an individual litigant or the member of a class) that arises from the other party's actions pursuant to this Security Instrument or that alleges that the other party has breached any provision of, or any duty owed by reason of, this Security Instrument, until such Borrower or Lender has notified the other party (with such notice given in compliance with the requirements of Section 15) of such alleged breach and afforded the other party hereto a reasonable period after the giving of such notice to take corrective action. If Applicable Law provides a time period which must elapse before certain action can be taken, that time period will be deemed to be reasonable for purposes of this paragraph. The notice of acceleration and opportunity to cure given to Borrower pursuant to Section 22 and the notice of acceleration given to Borrower pursuant to Section 18 shall be deemed to satisfy the notice and opportunity to take corrective action provisions of this Section 20.

21. Hazardous Substances. As used in this Section 21: (a) "Hazardous Substances" are those substances defined as toxic or hazardous substances, pollutants, or wastes by Environmental Law and the following substances: gasoline, kerosene, other flammable or toxic petroleum products, toxic pesticides and herbicides, volatile solvents, materials containing asbestos or formaldehyde, and radioactive materials; (b) "Environmental Law" means federal laws and laws of the jurisdiction where the Property is located that relate to health, safety or environmental protection; (c) "Environmental Cleanup" includes any response action, remedial action, or removal action, as defined in Environmental Law; and (d) an "Environmental Condition" means a condition that can cause, contribute to, or otherwise trigger an Environmental Cleanup.

Borrower shall not cause or permit the presence, use, disposal, storage, or release of any Hazardous Substances, or threaten to release any Hazardous Substances, on or in the Property. Borrower shall not do, nor allow anyone else to do, anything affecting the Property (a) that is in violation of any Environmental Law, (b) which creates an Environmental Condition, or (c) which, due to the presence, use, or release of a Hazardous Substance, creates a condition that adversely affects the value of the Property. The preceding two sentences shall not apply to the presence, use, or storage on the Property of small quantities of Hazardous Substances that are generally recognized to be appropriate to normal residential uses and to maintenance of the Property (including, but not limited to, hazardous substances in consumer products).

Borrower shall promptly give Lender written notice of (a) any investigation, claim, demand, lawsuit or other action by any governmental or regulatory agency or private party involving the Property and any Hazardous Substance or Environmental Law of which Borrower has actual knowledge, (b) any Environmental Condition, including but not limited to, any spilling, leaking, discharge, release or threat of release of any Hazardous Substance, and (c) any condition caused by the presence, use or release of a Hazardous Substance which adversely affects the value of the Property. If Borrower learns, or is notified by any governmental or regulatory authority, or any private party, that any removal or other remediation of any Hazardous Substance affecting the Property is necessary, Borrower shall promptly take all necessary remedial actions in accordance with Environmental Law. Nothing herein shall create any obligation on Lender for an Environmental Cleanup.

NON-UNIFORM COVENANTS. Borrower and Lender further covenant and agree as follows:

22. Acceleration; Remedies. Lender shall give notice to Borrower prior to acceleration following Borrower's breach of any covenant or agreement in this Security Instrument (but not prior to acceleration under Section 18 unless Applicable Law provides otherwise). The notice shall specify: (a) the default; (b) the action required to cure the default; (c) a date, not less than 30 days from the date the notice is given to Borrower, by which the default must be cured; and (d) that failure to cure the default on or before the date specified in the notice may result in acceleration of the sums secured by this Security Instrument and sale of the Property. The notice shall further inform Borrower of the right to reinstate after acceleration and the right to bring a court action to assert the non-existence of a default or any other defense of Borrower to acceleration and sale. If the default is not cured on or before the date specified in the notice, Lender at its option may require immediate payment in full of all sums secured by this Security Instrument without further demand and may invoke the power of sale granted by Borrower and any other remedies permitted by Applicable Law. Borrower appoints Lender the agent and attorney-in-fact for Borrower to exercise the power of sale. Lender shall be entitled to collect all expenses incurred in pursuing the remedies provided in this Section 22, including, but not limited to, reasonable attorneys' fees and costs of title evidence.

If Lender invokes the power of sale, Lender shall give a copy of a notice of sale by public advertisement for the time and in the manner prescribed by Applicable Law. Lender, without further demand on Borrower, shall sell the Property at public auction to the highest bidder at the time and place and under the terms designated in the notice of sale in one or more parcels and in any order Lender determines. Lender or its designee may purchase the Property at any sale.

23. Release. Upon payment of all sums secured by this Security Instrument, Lender shall cancel this Security Instrument. Borrower shall pay any recordation costs. Lender may charge Borrower a fee for releasing this Security Instrument, but only if the fee is paid to a third party for services rendered and the charging of the fee is permitted under Applicable Law.

24. Waiver of Homestead. Borrower waives all rights of homestead exemption in the Property.

25. Assumption Not a Novation. Lender's acceptance of an assumption of the obligations of this Security Instrument and the Note, and any release of Borrower in connection therewith, shall not constitute a novation.

26. Security Deed. This conveyance is to be construed under the existing laws of the State of Georgia as a deed passing title, and not as a mortgage, and is intended to secure the payment of all sums secured hereby.

BORROWER ACCEPTS AND AGREES to the terms and covenants contained in this Security Instrument and in any Rider executed by Borrower and recorded with it.

IN WITNESS WHEREOF, Borrower has signed and sealed this Security Instrument.

Signed, sealed and delivered in the presence of:

_____ _____ (Seal)
Unofficial Witness Best Buy Homes, LLC. - Borrower
By: Michael S. Cherwenka-Member

_____ _____ (Seal)
- Borrower
Notary Public, _____ County
_____

[Space Below This Line for Acknowledgment]

This is an example of a promissory note that you can use.

PROMISSORY NOTE-1078 ASHBY GROVE
January 20, 2017
Atlanta, Georgia

FOR VALUE RECEIVED, the undersigned, Best Buy Homes, LLC, (referred to herein as the "Borrower" or "Maker"), promises to pay to the order of **CKB HOMES, LLC.** (referred to herein as the "Lender" or "Holder"), at the mailing address of Lender – **2655Bethany Creek Ct.; Milton, Ga. 30034**, or at such other place as Holder shall designate from time to time in writing, the principal sum of **One Hundred Nineteen Thousand Dollars 00/100 ($119,000.00),** together with interest on the outstanding principal balance of this Note from the date hereof until fully paid at the interest rate of **ten percent (10%)** per annum, in lawful money of the United States of America, which shall at the time of payment be legal tender in payment of all debts. Paid at closing if proceeds are less than interest payments **$991.66 monthly.**

All principal and accrued interest hereunder shall be due and payable on or before January 20, 2018.

Payments shall be made to Holder at the address as stated above, or at such other place as the Holder hereof may designate in writing to the Borrower. The Borrower may prepay this Note in full or in part at any time without notice, penalty, prepayment fee, or payment of unearned interest. All payments hereunder received from the Borrower by the Holder shall be applied first to interest to the extent then accrued and then to principal, in inverse order of maturity.

The remedies of the Holder as provided herein and in any other documents governing or securing repayment hereof shall be cumulative and concurrent and may be pursued singly, successively, or together, at the sole discretion of the Holder, and may be exercised as often as occasion therefor shall arise.

The Borrower and all sureties, endorsers, and guarantors of this Note hereby (a) waive demand, presentment of payment, notice of nonpayment, protest, notice of protest and all other notice, filing of suit, and diligence in collecting this Note, or in enforcing any of its rights under any guaranties securing the repayment hereof; (b) agree to any substitution, addition, or release of any collateral or any party or person primarily or secondarily liable hereon; (c) agree that the Holder shall not be required first to institute any suit, or to exhaust his, their, or its remedies against the Borrower or any other person or party to become liable hereunder, or against any collateral in order to enforce payment of this Note; (d) consent to any extension, rearrangement, renewal, or postponement of time of payment of this Note and to any other indulgence with respect hereto without notice, consent, or consideration to any of them; and (e) agree that, notwithstanding the occurrence of any of the foregoing (except with the express written release by the Holder or any such person), they shall be and remain jointly and severally, directly and primarily, liable for all sums due under this Note.

Whenever used in this Note, the words "Borrower", "Maker" and "Holder" shall be deemed to include the Borrower and the Holder named in the opening paragraph of this Promissory Note, and their respective heirs, executors, administrators, legal representatives, successors, and assigns. It is expressly understood and agreed that the Holder shall never be construed for any purpose as a partner, joint venturer, co-principal, or associate of the Borrower, or of any person or party claiming by, through, or under the Borrower in the conduct of their respective businesses.

TIME IS OF THE ESSENCE OF THIS PROMISSORY NOTE.

This Note shall be construed and enforced in accordance with the laws of the State of Georgia.

The pronouns used herein shall include, when appropriate, either gender and both singular and plural, and the grammatical construction of sentences shall conform thereto.

All references herein to any document, instrument, or agreement shall be deemed to refer to such document, instrument, or agreement as the same may be amended, modified, restated, supplemented, or replaced from time to time.

NOTWITHSTANDING ANY PROVISION HEREOF TO THE CONTRARY, BORROWER'S PERSONAL LIABILITY FOR PAYMENT OF THIS NOTE AND PERFORMANCE OF THE OBLIGATIONS UNDER THIS NOTE ARE LIMITED TO THE PROPERTY AND LENDER SHALL NOT ENFORCE ANY LIABILITY OF BORROWER CREATED HEREUNDER AGAINST BORROWER OR ANY OF BORROWER'S PRINCIPALS, DIRECTORS, OFFICERS OR EMPLOYEES.

IN WITNESS WHEREOF, the undersigned Borrower has executed this instrument under seal as of the day and year first above written.

Best Buy Homes, LLC

_____ (Seal)

BY: Mike Cherwenka, Member

Self-Directed Individual Retirement Account (IRA)

A self-directed IRA is not a special type of IRA. The term *self-directed* refers to the way the account is administrated and the greater choice of investment options available to the account owner. More conventional retirement accounts involve a third party, such as a broker or other account administrator, who assists in the purchase of various publicly traded assets.

Self-directed IRAs are invested solely at the discretion of the owner of that account, who directs the account administrator (such as Advanta IRA) to purchase assets that are outside of the norm when it comes to retirement plans. Investment accounts that can be self-directed include traditional, Roth, SEP, and SIMPLE IRAs, as well as educational and health savings plans.

You can facilitate investments in real estate, private loans, private companies, and so on. You may simply look to your personal savings accounts to acquire these assets. However, you are allowed to use funds from a self-directed IRA to make these investments and more. By doing so, you may find a potentially large source of additional monies to make these different types of investments.

Self-directed IRA investments are secured by property and provide diversity in your retirement portfolio that can be safer than traditional investment vehicles and provide you with a higher rate of return on your investment portfolio. We are actively using our self-directed IRAs to fix and flip multiple properties. This type of funding vehicle has allowed us to return 20 percent to my portfolio each flip. Others have used their self-directed IRAs to hold the flip for years through rental income.

If you understand how to invest in real estate with a self-directed IRA, you gain the opportunity to earn tax-sheltered income for retirement on successful endeavors.

Real Estate

An investor can purchase vacant land and residential or commercial property with an IRA. Income (profits from a sale or rental proceeds) flows back to the IRA, tax-deferred. Expenses (such as property taxes, association maintenance dues, etc.) are paid by the IRA. Rehab properties, as well as properties in the foreclosure process, can be purchased as assets in an IRA.

Notes and Mortgages

Some investors use their IRAs to lend money to third parties. All loan payments (principal and interest) flow back into the IRA, tax-deferred. The majority of lending is safe, secured loans with the property used as collateral. An IRA can also loan money via an unsecured promissory note. Secured notes are backed by collateral, such as property and deeds of trust, providing additional assurance of the return of the loan amount and interest to the lender. Unsecured notes are not backed by collateral, and as such, constitute a higher risk—and sometimes reward—than a secured note.

Partnerships/LLCs

Individuals may want to make an IRA investment in conjunction with other investors. In many cases, the group of investors will form a partnership or LLC to make things easier to combine funds. The partnership or LLC can be formed for a number of reasons (holding real estate, making private loans, creating a private hedge fund, etc.), and the IRA can join as a partner in that entity. The IRA then shares in the profits and losses of the entity in accordance with its percentage of ownership. In most cases, the returns are not taxable to the IRA, although depending on the type and purpose of the entity, the IRA may be subject to unrelated business income tax.

Rental Property Assets

Rental property can also be purchased using an IRA. This alternative asset could potentially present growth if higher interest rates prevent people from purchasing homes—because they have to live somewhere and renting a home or condo may be their only option.

Your self-directed IRA can purchase houses, apartment buildings, duplexes, and more. Income is obviously earned via rent payments, which can offer a steady return on your investment over time.

Real estate is an asset that many believe stands the test of time and survives the harshest conditions of the American economy. Historically, property value appreciates over time, and if you have time on your side, the above options may be advantageous to your portfolio.

Advanta IRA manages our self-directed IRA. You may find the questions below frequently asked questions that Advanta receives from investors:

Who owns the property purchased by my self-directed IRA?

Your IRA owns the property, not you. All documents, legal or otherwise (including the offer, contract, and title), must be written to reflect the IRA's ownership of the real estate asset.

Can my IRA partner with someone or borrow money to purchase real estate?

Your IRA may partner with another IRA, person, or entity. Provided the partner is not a disqualified person, pooling funds to invest in real estate this way eliminates the need for acquiring other loans, increases purchasing power and lowers the risk factors that are present with any investment.

Can I perform repairs or maintenance on real estate in my IRA?

No. Doing so would be considered "sweat equity" and a contribution to your account. Sweat equity cannot be measured in value, and the IRS only permits contributions to a self-directed IRA to be made in cash. Repairs and maintenance must be paid for at current market rates and must be performed by a third party who is not a disqualified person.

Do I have to hire someone to manage the property?

No. Property management can be handled by the IRA owner, but you must not perform sweat equity or pay for expenses out of your own pocket. You can also hire a third party property manager if you wish. All income and expenses flow directly in and out of the IRA funds, not your own.

How are income and expenses attributed to my IRA?

All income and expenses associated with the real estate investment must flow directly in and out of your IRA. Rent checks and other income must be written to the IRA and deposited directly into the self-directed IRA account. Expenses must be paid by the IRA and not by you personally. Income or expenses are not allowed to flow through the IRA owner for any reason. It is crucial that you plan for any expenses in advance, so your IRA is prepared to cover them. If you have partnered on a purchase with other parties, your IRA only pays for its percentage of repairs and must receive only its share of income.

Can I sell property to my IRA?

Your IRA is not allowed to purchase real estate from you or from another disqualified person. Your IRA is also not allowed to sell the property to you or a disqualified person. Such actions are deemed prohibited transactions and could cause your IRA to suffer heavy penalties or even disqualification.

Can I vacation in the rental property owned by my IRA?

No. Investments made by your IRA are to be realized at your retirement and not before. You (or any disqualified person) are not allowed to utilize the real estate investment in any manner. For example, if you have purchased a rental property in a popular vacation area, you may not vacation in that property. Doing so would be deemed as your receiving a current benefit and can cause penalties or disqualification of your self-directed.

Hard Money Loans

According to Wikipedia, "A hard money loan is a specific type of asset-based loan financing through which a borrower receives funds secured by the value of a parcel of real estate." In short, a hard money loan is an asset-backed loan, not unlike a traditional mortgage, that is a common tool for real estate investors. Hard money loans allow you to purchase an investment property with less cash out of pocket.

- 3 points or $3,500 minimum (for example, it will cost a buyer $3,600 to borrow $120,000)
- 13 percent interest
- 65 percent loan-to-value
- 20 percent down

The money in most cases is expensive, but it's not the cost of the money—it's the availability. Hard money lenders are a great security blanket for new investors because they inspect the property to verify estimates and validate the after-repair value (ARV) and cost of repairs. In other words, your hard money lenders can help you avoid getting in bad deals because they are a second set of due diligence eyes for you. Even if you currently don't need a hard money lender for an upcoming project, it's a good idea to keep a few in your back pocket.

Action Step: Identify two hard money lenders:

Crowdfunding for Real Estate Projects

Crowdfunding means financing a product, idea, or venture using small amounts of money raised from the "crowd," or members of the public. Typically, crowdfunding associated with a large number of individual investors or donors. It initially started when entrepreneurs or organizations would turn to the crowd to raise funds for projects needing funding.

Funding would come in the form of donations, though platforms would occasionally offer rewards for different donation levels. Kickstarter, Indiegogo, and Tilt are all examples of donation- and rewards-based crowdfunding platforms.

Being successful in startup fundraising via crowdfunding is not as easy as it seems. It comes with a lot of effort and dedication, but if one puts in the necessary work, one can realize fortunes that go far beyond just the raising of money. Crowdfunding is a possible alternative way to fund a venture, and it can be done without giving up equity or accumulating debt. Real estate investors who want to increase the diversity of their portfolio can leverage crowdfunding to gain the exposure to make that happen. Check out www.fundrise.com, ww.realtymogul.com, and other crowdfunding providers where you can learn more

We have not taken advantage of this investing platform, so talk to various investors to learn their pros and cons of using this option.

Private Mortgage Loan

We have deals that are funded by private mortgage loans investors with various professional backgrounds who don't want active roles in our projects.

Note: Private mortgage loan is not like hard money lenders, whose fees can eat up a majority of your profit. Hard money lenders are useful for investors and others who have a hard time getting approved. They are often more expensive than other mortgages and require low LTV ratios.

When we set up our private mortgage loan, ensure that it's a win-win for both parties with minimal risk. The flyer on the next page is what we use to effectively attract real estate private mortgage lenders.

CHAPTER 7

Launch Your Real Estate Career With No Money

No bees, no honey; no work, no money.

—Proverb

Haven't you always wanted to be a bird dog?

What's a Bird Dog

A person who spends his or her time locating properties that meet the ARV requirements. In real estate investing, properties are often purchased in less than great condition, with the plan to make repairs or remodel them and resell or flip them at a profit. When we look at the viability of a project, we estimate the value of the property after all repairs are completed, or the after-value. Determining ARV requires the ability to gather repair estimates with accuracy and insight.

Most successful bird dogs have spent years, or even decades, working in and around real estate and have developed their instincts about a property's potential. If you want to be successful in the bird dog field, the wisest best step is to work for a more seasoned investor.

Bird Dog Role

The assignor finds a property a seller is willing to sell significantly below market value and then resell that property to another buyer, normally a real estate investor, at a higher price. Typically, the bird dog profits $2,000–$4,000 per transaction.

Bird Dog's Customers

Me. Make one call: 770-365-4997. That's all.

If you're not in the region where I focus, go to your local real estate investment group to find cash heavy real estate investors. We have several bird dogs who bring us deals on a regular basis. Our criterion is simple:

The ARV is 60–65 percent.

Protect Yourself

Prior to bringing any deals to an investor, obtain the payment arrangement in writing. Following is a bird dog contract that you can use as a reference; however, this is not a substitution for legal advice.

Bird Dog Agreement

This Agreement is made effective as of _____, 20__, by and between _____("hereinafter "Buyer" or "Seller" [circle one]), of_____, and_____, of_____.
In this Agreement, the parties who are contracting to receive services shall be referred to as the "Seller" or the "Buyer" [circle one], and the party who will be providing the services shall be referred to as the "Consultant". The Seller and/or the Buyer desire to have services provided by the Consultant. Therefore, the parties agree as follows:

1. DESCRIPTION OF SERVICES. Beginning on _____, 20__, the Consultant will provide the following services (collectively, the "Services"): a real estate, locator, referral and contact service.

2. PERFORMANCE OF SERVICES. The Consultant shall determine the manner in which the Services are to be performed and the specific hours to be worked by the Consultant. The Seller and/or the Buyer will rely on The Consultant to work as many hours as may be reasonably necessary to fulfill the Consultant's obligations under this Agreement.

3. 3. PAYMENT. The Seller, through the Buyer, will pay a locator, referral and/or contact fee to the Consultant for the Services

equivalent to $_____ (_____%) of the total proceeds derived from the sale and/or purchase of the certain property located, referred and/or contacted as requested by Seller and/or Buyer, or a flat fee in the amount of $_____ for services as described in Paragraph 1 above. All fees due to Consultant shall be payable in a lump sum upon completion of the Services unless otherwise further negotiated between the Seller and/or the Buyer and the Consultant. Upon termination of this Agreement, payments under this paragraph shall cease; provided, however, that the Consultant shall be entitled to payments for periods or partial periods that occurred prior to the date of termination and for which the Consultant has not yet been paid.

4. TERM/TERMINATION. This Agreement shall terminate automatically upon completion by the Consultant of the Services required by this Agreement.

5. RELATIONSHIP OF PARTIES. It is understood by the parties that the Consultant is an Independent contractor with respect to each, and not an employee of either. Neither the Seller's and/or Buyer's business shall provide fringe benefits, including health insurance benefits, paid vacation, or any other employee benefit, for the benefit of the Consultant under this Agreement.

6. EMPLOYEES. The Consultant's employees, if any, who perform services for the Seller and/or Buyer under this Agreement, shall also be bound by the provisions of this Agreement. At the request of either the Seller or the Buyer, the Consultant shall provide adequate evidence that such persons are the Consultant's employees.

Steps to Becoming a Successful Bird Dog

Step 1: Find a motivated seller.

A motivated seller is an individual who has to sell a property quickly. There is a huge disparity between want to sell and need to sell. Knowing which category your seller falls into is the first step in identifying how to handle the situation. To understand the motivation of a buyer, ask why he or she is selling.

Sample *Need* to Sell Responses

- This house is getting more and more difficult to maintain. It requires tons or repairs, but I don't have the money.
- I am so sick of these stressful renters. I'm ready to get rid of my rental property and retire.

Sample *Want* to Sell Responses

- I am thinking about selling my house in the next year. Do you know how much my house is worth?
- My renters are working out, but I am thinking about selling my rentals in the next six to nine months.

Step 2: Get the contract.

There are many assignment contract templates on the web. However, you must have an attorney to review and approve contract template you select. Leveraging the services of an attorney will provide you with the comfort and confidence knowing your assignment contract is legal. Additionally, you will be able to utilize that attorney as counsel in the event you find yourself in litigation. It's critical that your assignment contract contains the clause "and/or assigns." This clause authorizes you to trade the property to another buyer who is interested in the property. When you receive the executed contract, you now have an equitable interest in the property and legal standing in what happens to the property.

Step 3: Submit contract to closing attorney or title company.

This process may differ in each state, but there is normally either a title company or a closing attorney who will conduct a title search. The title search will check the historical records of the property to make sure there are no liens on the property. The title company or the closing attorney is an independent third party hired to make sure the deal is fair as agreed upon in the contract. Additionally, get title insurance in case a defect in the title is discovered later

Step 4: Find your buyer and assign the contract.

If you're in the southeast, contact me to see if it meets criteria. Other great sources to sell your deals are Craigslist.com, Zillow.com, Trulia.com, and similar.

Have the buyer give nonrefundable earnest money as it will become yours even if the transaction does not close. The earnest money can be as much or as little you require within reason. Assignments range from hundreds to thousands. When the buyer deposits the earnest money, you know that you produced a willing, able and ready buyer who has a real interest in the property and is willing to move forward.

Get Paid!

This is what most of us want to hear. We get paid when the end buyer wires in the funds for the deal. This money will cover what you stated you were willing to buy the property from the seller for, as well as your fee for facilitating the transaction. As an example, if you told the seller you would buy the house for $50,000 and you then sold your interest in the property to the buyer for $52,500, then your assignment fee is $2,500. It is standard practice that assignments are done only on profits of $5,000 or below. But if you are comfortable with the seller and the buyer, it's possible to assign a contract for a much higher fee.

Have you ever heard the invitations on radio or TV to seminars and conferences with the tagline, "Get rich in real estate with no money down"? When you get to the event, some speaker is discussing how he became rich as a wholesaler with no money. Unfortunately, that is a tactic to fill seats and sell you books, tapes, and software that you won't ever use. To prove that wholesaling is not the entry point into real estate investing, I would like for you to name three people you personally know who is a successful wholesaler, buying and selling at least two homes per month who does not have cash:

Over the years, we have attended or presented at countless seminars where they tell you the first entry point into real estate is to become a wholesaler because it doesn't require money to get started. In theory, that is absolutely true. It can happen in the role of a bird dog.

Finding a deal is great, but if you do not have earnest money to tie up a deal or funds to purchase it, then all that time and effort looking for a great property is for nothing.

When you make an offer on a property, it is usually required that you provide an earnest money deposit—typically a minimum of $1,000 or 10 percent of the purchase price—with your offer. If you are currently living paycheck-to-paycheck, coming up with even a few hundred dollars can be a big hurdle in launching your real estate investment business, let alone thousands needed for a purchase.

Challenges of the Bird Dog Role

During various real estate transactions as a bird dog, you *will* face the following challenges:

- The seller unwilling to sign assignable contracts
- Contract assignment cannot be done on *most* of the transactions available—HUD homes, REOs, institutional sellers
- Listed properties present many barriers when trying to perform this type of transaction because it's public information
- Title restrictions that require ninety-day seasoning
- The sellers in the area that you're targeting have heard it all before so they only want buyers who can close quickly with cash, only
- It most likely will take years to become successful
- Most sellers require proof of funds

STEP 3—HOW TO FIND THE RIGHT PROPERTY

CHAPTER 8

How to Buy in Area with the Highest Returns

Real estate cannot be lost or stolen, nor can it be taken away. Purchased with common sense, paid in full, managed with reasonable care, it's the safest investment in the world.

—Franklin D. Roosevelt

Most people want to purchase a property in the cool places that are a couple of blocks from the "up-and-coming neighborhood." That's why those zip codes are saturated with real estate investors who are driving the prices beyond the 65 percent loan-to-value ratio that is needed to be successful in real estate investing. I have experienced tons of success investing in properties in the low-risk zip codes. In other words, my properties are a few blocks from the hood. Most importantly, as a real estate investor, I know the properties in my zip codes like the back of my hand; that is, days on the market, the pride of the community, target buyers, upcoming commercial developments, and buyer's design preference. The pyramid below depicts our target buying area.

The Hunt – Find the Property

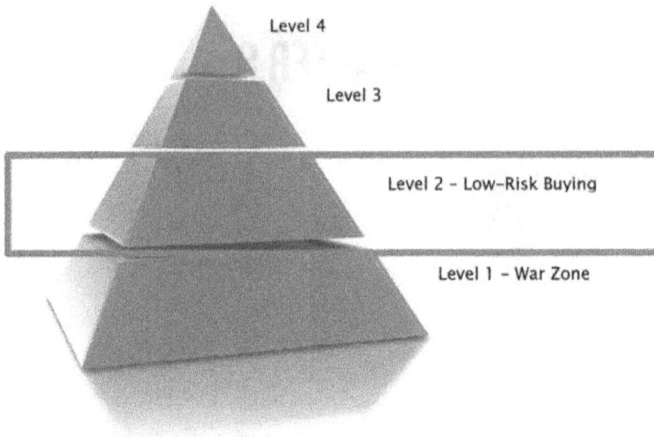

Level 4

Level 3

Level 2 – Low–Risk Buying

Level 1 – War Zone

Our best recommendation is that you work with someone who has the means to close a real estate transaction quickly, like Mike, for example. We encourage you to work with experienced wholesalers. You can find them through real estate investment associations and referrals.

Action Steps: Identity two experienced wholesalers that you are going to work with. *We took the liberty of filling out the first one for you.*

GoldmineProperties.net/mcherwenka@aol.com

Other great sources are real estate owned properties on MLS, auctions, estate sales, and courthouse steps.

Real estate investing workshops will tell you to place bandit signs, call on for-sale-by-owner properties, and send flyers. You may stumble across a few nuggets here and there, but in reality, you will never build a large portfolio of properties. Some real estate investors won't tell you that building a database of buyers and sellers is grassroots and a slow process. Mike built his massive database of distressed sellers by staying networking in the real estate investing associations and working with bird dogs.

Paralysis of analysis is the reason people don't progress beyond this step. Don't overthink the deal. When I am presented with a great buy on a property, I spend fifteen minutes or less analyzing the deal.

Question to Ask Yourself When Finding a Property

Is it in my target area?

We renovate houses in areas that some would consider the hood of Atlanta, Decatur, Stone Mountain, and similar areas. However, there is a bit of magic to selecting the right house on the right street in distressed areas, because one block can be high risk compared to another that is on the next street. That's why we hold steadfast to the belief that if you have not been a bird dog or a skin-in wholesaler for a decade or more in your target area, you are gravely at risk to having an unsellable property.

Do the purchase price and repairs add up to 65 percent loan-to-value or less?

After flipping more than 2,100 houses over that last twenty-one years, we can walk in a house and within minutes know the total cost of repairs. If you are a novice at repairs, have three honest general contractors walk you through a thorough breakdown of fixes. Toss out the highest and lowest bid to get a good feel for what you will be spending. Keep in mind that you will encounter unknown latent defects in older homes. That why it is best to have a 5 percent cost overrun bucket.

TOP SECRET

Cherwenkas Pocket Flipping Method - flip houses in the same pocket so your own flips will be your comp in the appraisal.

Does the independent appraisal validate my ARV?

We spend several hours comparing sold properties within a two-mile radius of our rehab, the single best tool to determine a home's value, to obtain a comparable, contract criteria from recently sold properties in a neighborhood such as sales price, square footage, house age, and floor plan. We make offers based on those findings. After our offer is accepted, we pay a certified appraiser to verify our comparable research. Since we specialize in certain zip codes, there are always a few of our fix-and-flip sales in the appraisal.

Are there few boarded-up houses?

Some investors buy a house if it's in their target area and 65 percent on the dollar. That approach doesn't work if there are lots of boarded-up houses on the street. We don't follow a specific formula about the number of vacant houses that are acceptable. To determine how many vacant houses don't feel right, walk the street. If you feel uneasy or like Freddy Krueger is going to jump out and stab you at any moment, then your buyer will most likely feel the same way. I am sure you're like, *"Feel?* What the heck am I to do with that!" That's why am I a broken record about working with a skin-in investor to avoid worrying about *feel*.

Is there minimal foot traffic?

Does it look like the street is used as a pass-through to a store, drug dealer? Foot traffic is a major ingredient in a recipe for high crime or violence.

Other considerations that we make when selecting a flip

- Is the home 1,200 square ft or larger?
- Does it have at least three beds and two baths? If not, is there space to add a bath? Most buyers don't want a two bed/two bath, because it reminds them of an apartment
- Are the neighbors keeping their houses up? Flower beds, roofs repaired, and grass cut.

If the responses to the aforementioned questions are yes, write an offer *now*! Inquiring about anything else is a total waste of your brain power.

CHAPTER 9

Benefits of Flipping a House

The house you looked at today and wanted to think about until tomorrow may be the same house someone looked at yesterday and will buy today!

—Koki Adasi

Over the years, we have jokingly said that real estate is the most lucrative thing that you can do that's legal. This is the number-one reason we got involved in house flipping. The profits are large and quick. Like any high-profit business, there are risks.

TOP SECRET

Negotiate with online and big box retailers to get them to beat each other prices!

Money isn't the only benefit associated with flipping real estate, but it's definitely the primary motivator for investors when they get into house flipping.

Let's discuss the meat and potatoes—the profit.

Investors get into real estate for the profit. Most are unaware that the work is difficult. Renovating houses isn't a cakewalk, and it's definitely not the type of work you would usually undertake for the simple love of getting your hands dirty. This is real work that leaves you bone weary at the end of the day.

When Mike got into real estate in 1996, he used day laborers and his sweat equity to renovate his houses. Prior to Mike's first flip, he was a successful international entertainer who was used to wealth and success. His walk with God was the reason he left the entertainment industry, so he truly stepped out on faith and passion for succeeding.

Each day, Mike would go the Petro gas station on Donald Lee Holloway Parkway (formerly known as Bankhead Hwy) in Atlanta, Georgia, to get a laborer based on the task that he had that day. He worked around the clock, taking small breaks to sleep on the floor of the rehab and showering at the gas station. Sweat equity can be difficult on your project if you have a nine-to-five job, but we suggest that you assign some of the renovation tasks to yourself. If you don't think you can do any task, sign up for Home Depot, Lowe's, and other home renovation retailers that provide free education for renovation projects. This will allow you to learn the complexity, duration, effort, and cost of rehab task from firsthand experience; as a result, when you grow your flipping business and start using general contractor estimates you have a better understanding of true cost

The Payoff

When all the work's done and you make the sale, you'll find that the profit involved in a successful house flip is well worth the effort you've put into the entire process. Your earnings can exceed most people yearly salary after a couple of projects.

Please receive and accept this information: flips *will go wrong*, so expect the unexpected, but if you're prepared and wise, they won't ruin or end your career. You can still turn a profit, even when things fall apart.

Other Benefits of Flipping Houses

You are working for yourself. You don't have to punch a time clock or request vacation days off or unpaid overtime because you're on a salary.

Tolla worked from home for the largest IT company in the world. She would often say that her company had a difficult time finding engineers who are willing to work from home because the applicants say they lack the discipline to stay focused at home forty hours a week. While you're making the decision to transition into real estate investing full-time, ask yourself if will you get distracted washing dishes, clothes, your hair, or social networking, surfing the Internet, and so on. Truthfully, if you work a nine-to-five and you spend lots of time at the water cooler, roaming around, and so on, most likely, you will have to put lots of processes in place to control your wandering mind and body.

Although this business requires a lot of work in order to see a significant ROI, there's some satisfaction at the end of the day in knowing that you're working for yourself and not making someone else wealthy by chasing their dreams instead of yours. That feeling of satisfaction is one that you should hang onto when the brand-new appliance you just installed catches on fire or an exterior unexpectedly falls a week after you close because of termites.

House flipping is tough, and it will mostly be the most frustrating type of investments you can pursue. As you grow in the flipping business, it will be one of the most rewarding things you can do financially, spiritually, and mentally. Most importantly, find passion in flipping. Don't solely focus on the financial gain. We love the large checks that we receive, but we love the impact our work has on the community. We are able to give jobs to the unemployable in our working areas. Additionally, we have contractors on our staff that include a father, son, mother, brother-in-law, nephew, and son-in-law. That gives us great pride and accomplishment, knowing that we're providing a stable career for generations of families.

After each closing, we give a minimum of 10 percent back. In the picture above, delivering our yearly supply of new blankets, coats, toiletries, and other essentials to the homeless.

CHAPTER 10

Mike's Story about His First Flip

Later in the book, we are going to focus on my role as a successful skin-in wholesaler. Meanwhile, I hope you can learn from when I purchased my first two flips. The wholesaler I purchased my properties from was the hard money lender also. He falsified the appraisal and repairs estimate. Duh, right? Why didn't I see that coming! I went from no money to $100,000 in debt.

When you are a newbie, you have a target on your back. There are people who see you coming, and they simply can't wait to devour you. That's why you trust but verify. I can't blame the investor for taking advantage of my inexperience, because I should have done my own due diligence.

To help you lower the risk of becoming a target, we put together some quick tips to remember:

- Get a certified appraisal.
- Get three contractor estimates.
- Develop a budget from the three estimates.
- Don't pay contractors until the tasks are 100 percent complete.
- Pay for your own material. When subs go to Home Depot's pro desk to check out, I read all of my receipts to see if contractors and

subs are buying personal items, tools, and unusual quantities. If everything checks out, I pay via their text-alert system.

- Perform a visual inspection of the task. We paid a plumber for completing the task of installing the plumbing fixtures and all of the connections. A few days later, we realized that he had dropped the fixtures into the sinks and had not connected in the crawl space.
- Track expenses. This is a simple tracking form that you can start using in a spreadsheet:

Task	Planned Cost	Actual Cost	Expected Completion Date	Actual Completion Date

It's important to record your project in a spreadsheet or database so you can measure how you are improving on cost, quality, and time-to-market. Technology is the key to managing your project and accounting business functions. In order for your business to scale, the business must understand where it is performing well and where it needs improvement. As many as 50 percent of my customers are repeat buyers. Some of them have purchased as many of fifteen homes from me since 2011 because they *make money*.

CHAPTER 11

What Features of the House Matter Most in Flip?

If you focus on results, you will never change. If you focus on change, you will get results.

—Jack Dixon

An investor working a few streets over from me cut corners and did what amounted to a kindergarten rehab. Then he couldn't figure out why we sold three houses as his flip sat on the market for months. People in all zip codes know quality, and in this era of home-flipping television and home-improvement websites, the expectations are even higher than in previous decades. Analyze the properties of flippers that sell quickly in the zip codes and price points that you're operating.

One Action Step: Identify three properties you are going to analyze

There are some quick tips to not over- or underimprove the rehab project and ensure a quick sale. Let's go room by room:

All of the homes in the photos below are for first time homebuyers ($200K and below). We believe in giving high quality and design for an affordable price.

Paint

- We paint our color a pale gray in most of the house.
- We paint a spa color in the master bath soft blue and the master tray ceiling the same tranquil colors.

Mike and Tolla have go-big-or-go-home personalities, so they take design risks. In the photo below, they use black to highlight the massive raised ceiling, trim, and doors. We recommend that you go with neutral colors in your flip.

Before

After

In the after photo above, you can see that we don't play it safe with he use of bold dark colors. Newbies or the unsure should stick with natural colors.

Before

In general, paint smaller rooms in softer, lighter colors to help make the room feel larger. To make a room appear to be bigger than it is, paint it the same color as the adjacent room. If you have a small kitchen and dining room, a seamless look will make both rooms feel like one big space. And make a sunporch look bigger and more inviting by painting it green to reflect the color of nature. If you're staging your rehab and you want to create the illusion of more space, paint the walls the same color as your drapery. It will give you a seamless and sophisticated look. Some people use virtual staging services for the photos. We like the buyer to feel as if he or she just needs a toothbrush when they walk into our homes. Paint colors can *kill* a deal. If you're unsure, seek expert help.

The Kitchen

Don't skimp on the kitchen design. It's the heart of the home. Most of our residential rehabs target first-time homebuyers. Some investors think that you can go cheap with this market and they still will buy. That simply is a losing way of thinking. The average first-time homebuyers in our working areas are living in luxury apartments, so they are accustomed to nice finishes. We kick it up a couple notches from what they expect to make our money fast so we can move onto the next project. A flipping model that cuts costs and corners is doomed to fail. Keep in mind that a kitchen remodel is a 50–85 percent ROI.

Before

Before

After

Decisions, Decisions—Keep or Reface?

Whether your rehab includes a kitchen spruce-up or a complete overhaul, deciding what to do about your cabinets is one of the biggest decisions you'll make. New cabinets can take up nearly 50 percent of your total kitchen renovation budget, and functional cabinets can mean the difference between a kitchen that works and one that doesn't. But what if you can't afford to buy all-new cabinet on your rehab budget.

Three Reface Options

There are three primary ways to reface cabinets:

1. Refinish or paint existing cabinet and drawer fronts.
2. Install new wood or laminate veneer over existing cabinet and drawer fronts.
3. Install completely new cabinet doors and drawer fronts.

Deciding which of these three options to choose comes down to budget. Do as much as you budget will allow. When refacing the cabinets, consider freshening up the interiors too. They can be sanded, painted or veneered for a completely new look. Cabinet refacing can save up to 50 percent compared to the cost of replacing them and much less involved process than removing old cabinets and installing new ones.

Even with the potential cost-savings, however, refacing isn't right for every kitchen remodel. If they are not high-quality cabinets to begin with or they're extremely worn out, it is best to replace them. Because the kitchen is the heart of the home, we replace the cabinets in 97 percent of our rehabs.

Knocking Down Interior Walls

To give the house a more open look and make it more inviting for entertainment, remove the walls that aren't needed for privacy. Our rule of thumb is to remove it if it doesn't hide a bathroom or bedroom. You can see significant returns on using header kits that are needed create that open look.

Before

After

Master Bedroom

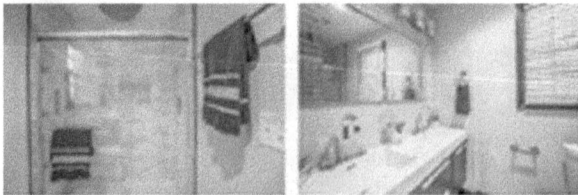

A master bedroom with a fresh look not only feels good but also gives you an ROI between 40 and 80 percent.

Expanded closets and larger master bathrooms are the top features homeowners want in their new bedroom suite. We are replacing old tubs with tiled showers, overhead shower sprays, and custom body spray systems.

A well-done new bathroom in your master suite will always give you a good return on your investment. Budget permitting, add closet system (the big box home renovation stores and online retailers have affordable options) to your closet roomy closet to seal the deal.

Before and After Master Bathroom View from Bedroom

Don't Forget to Look Up—Dress the Ceiling.

The age of the distressed houses we renovate range between 1900 and 1960. People love classic historic homes tastefully blended with modern features. If missing, we always tray the ceiling, recessed lights, crown molding, and sometimes special ceiling treatments or colors in the recessed part of the tray. If popcorn ceilings exist in the master, remove them; that's nonnegotiable.

Before   **After**

Curb Appeal Simple Recommendations

- Create flower beds with berms.
- Plant colorful. We plant lots of plants to make the buyer feel at home.

- Add solar light fixtures.
- Add large exteriors numbers.

- Update front door a bright color.
- If the driveway is heavily cracked, budget in a replacement. Most of the time you can get away with a concrete overlay. Always ask a few experts for the most affordable option. Driveways can get extremely expensive.
- We always build or significantly remodel the deck. Most people play it safe with a nice stained color. We're building more modern houses so the go with black or other colors that push the envelope in a positive way.
- Flat roof line? Add A-frame elevation or jazz up the elevation with a wraparound porch. No one wants a house that looks like it's straight out of Bedrock.

Before

Before

After

Before

After

Floors

- Carpet versus hardwood debate: Most buyers today don't want carpet in the house at all. We use real hardwoods even though out buyers are first time because we believe in providing our buyers with an Armand de Brignac Brut Gold Champagne (the most expensive champagne in the world, at $7,000 per bottle) finishes on their beer budget. If your rehab budget doesn't permit hardwoods and tile throughout, use carpet secondaries and a quality laminate wood.

Before   **After**

- Flooring that is at the entry or foyer of your rehab should have a "wow" factor, but be durable to outdoor elements. Flooring in bedrooms and kids' rooms should be comfortable for bare feet. Flooring in utility, laundry, and bathrooms should be able to resist water. Hardwood and laminate wood flooring is not recommended in areas of high moisture, as warping and damage can occur.
- Flooring is priced per square foot and can add up quickly! All flooring materials have "grades" of quality. Synthetic carpet is cheaper than Berber carpet that contains big and small tufts of pile. The plusher or more durable the carpet, naturally, the more expensive it will be. When choosing carpet, don't forget to select a carpet pad that will make your steps feel plush. Ceramic, slate, and marble tile is generally more expensive than carpet. Tile is very low maintenance and doesn't usually have to be replaced unless it cracks. Wood and laminate flooring have become more affordable over the years, due to new products entering the flooring market.

STEP 5—STAGING

CHAPTER 12

Decorating with Style

If bad decorating was a hanging offense, there would be bodies hanging from every tree!

—Sylvester Stallone

Furniture Placement for the Average Buyer is a Challenge

Staging is a must-have task in your project plan. Tolla is the stager in chief for our company. After we married and merged households, we had tons of furniture left over; so, we used it to stage our houses.

If design is your weakness, check with the local real estate investing groups for affordable staging options. When you interview for stagers, ask for a portfolio to see if their work will appeal to the buyers in your zip code, check the quality and condition of stager's furniture and the days-on-market for the houses that they stage.

Quality furniture that is perfectly placed can take a quality rehab to the next level. The buyers should imagine themselves packing up a toothbrush and settling in. Our company is passionate about staging. That's why we provide that service to investors who purchase wholesale deals from us and list with us.

Below is a collection of tips to stage if you want to save money and stage your own house:

Cleanliness Is Next to Godliness

- No matter how much money you spend on staging, if the house isn't clean, it won't sell. When you put the rehab on the market, clean it from top to bottom: ceiling fans, blinds, and windowsills. Shiny floors, kitchen and baths sparkling, door knobs and handles glistening, signal to the buyer that you take pride in your rehab and it creates the first layer of trust. Prepare for your rehab to get dirty during showing by budgeting or set aside your personal time to thoroughly clean weekly. Disperse plugins in the various living spaces.

Before

After

Peekaboo Is Not for You

- Never let the potential buyer(s) see the rehab before you're complete and the homes are staged. Small undone items may completely freak them. It's best to have everyone wait for the listing date to generate as many offers as possible.

Before   **After**

Stage a Little or Stage It All?

- Stage the living room, dining room, and a master bedroom. Add accessories to the kitchen and bathrooms. Add outdoor patio furniture to visually extend the living space.

Be a Magician.

- Use decorative mirrors to expand the room by adding instant light to the living space. For larger rooms or any room with a more limited amount of natural light, mirrors placed directly across from the windows will add instant light. Mixing and matching large and small mirrors on a wall in an interesting pattern is a great and inexpensive way to showcase art walls and spread light.

Get Off the Wall.

- There's a common belief that rooms will feel larger if all the furniture is pushed against the walls, but that isn't the case. Instead, furnish the space by floating furniture away from walls, even in small spaces. Reposition sofas and chairs into cozy conversational groups so the buyer can imagine entertaining.

Bring the Warmth

- Throw rugs add warmth, texture, comfort, color, and personality to the living space. It makes the buyers want to sit down and kick their shoes off.

Light Their Way

- One of the things that make staged homes look so warm and welcoming is great lighting. Most homes need extra light. To remedy the problem, add lots of table lamps and put them on a timer.

Reuse and Remind

- Instead of buying staging furniture as we did, take a good look at what you already have. Trays—wooden, acrylic, metal, or silver—can be placed on top of luggage racks, tea carts, trunks, bedside tables, and coffee tables for extra texture and dimension. Arrange candles on them, frames or pile books on top of them. You will be amazed at what you can do with what you can repurpose.

TOP SECRET

Know What Style Fits Your Community!

Our area is teeming with young professionals who love a modern aesthetic, so until the communities we invest in shift in design, we will keep running with our sleek, modern look.

STEP 6 - SELECTING AN AGENT

CHAPTER 13

Insights into Successful Real Estate Agents

Two real estate agents decided to start a new career to sell shoes. The two real estate agents go to Africa to open up new markets. Three days after arriving, one real estate agent said, "I'm returning on the next flight. Can't sell shoes here. Everybody goes barefoot."

At the same time, the other real estate agent sent an email to the factory, telling "The prospects are unlimited. Nobody wears shoes here!"

Real Estate Agents Representative, Select Wisely

All agents are not created equal. A good agent can make the process of selling your rehab go nicely, or a fabulous agent can make it go effortlessly. The most important need you have from the listing agent is to get the home sold quickly, at the full listing price, and with few concessions. Our listing team avoids the risk of pricing too high or too low by getting a certified appraisal. Your passion will be in this rehab, so that will most likely cause you to think your flip is worth more than the market will support based on comparable homes in the area. That's right; even if you find a buyer who is willing, able, and ready to purchase your rehab but it doesn't appraise, it will cause unnecessary disappointment.

A few things to consider when looking for an agent

- How well does the agent know the neighborhood and type of buyers? How many sells and or listings has he or she had in your target area over the last year?
- Create a communication plan with the agent that includes frequency and type of updates that you will receive.
- Look for evidence that the agent has a waiting list of buyers of agents by making them what's the average days on the market for the listings in your rehabs' neighborhood.
- Ask them for a marketing plan (e.g., social media, MLS, open houses).

The agent will be your partner; thus, outstanding character and the ability to effectively communicate is imperative. Agents who are strategic, charismatic and well-spoken can pull a crumbling contract back together.

Accepting Offers

It's imperative that you vet your buyer before accepting offers. We only accept preapproval not prequalification because the buyer who is preapproved is further in the loan qualification process. To further reduce the risk of the loan falling through, we call the lender to see if the buyer has submitted most of the important paperwork, like tax returns, pay stubs, and bank statements. Additionally, we ask the lender if it is confident that the buyer will clear underwriting process.

CHAPTER 14

The Greater Fool Theory Kills Deals

A greedy person is the poorest person in the world.

—Nicolas Chamfort

Trying to price your home too high because you spent x dollars on your rehab, or because it's a labor of love, is a sure way to stall the successful sale of your property. Buyers don't care that you need x amount of dollars for the sale of your flip. It's your fault that you lost control of change orders or you paid too much for material.

TOP SECRET

All a buyer cares about is paying the fair market, not your cost overruns!

According to Wikipedia, "The greater fool theory states that the price of an object is determined not by its intrinsic value, but rather by irrational beliefs and expectations of market participants. A price can be justified by a rational buyer under the belief that another party is willing to pay an even higher price. In other words, one may pay a price that seems 'foolishly' high because one may rationally have the expectation that the item can be resold to a 'greater fool' later."

Ensure that your emotions are not setting the price by ordering an independent appraisal. The moment you want to set the price at what you *feel* if the right price, you're setting yourself up for failure. Greed will cause you to scare off the best buyers before you ever get a chance to show them your home. The rehab will become undesirable. The strategy of dropping the price will highlight inexperience and cause buyers' agents not to take your rehab seriously.

Don't get us wrong: you can sell your home for more than the appraised value when you deliver a rehab that exceeds the buyer's expectations. The majority of our homes receive multiple offers because we price right! Several of these went well beyond our asking price after we called for highest and best offers. On the next page, we documented some of our rehabs to show that we always get asking price or above.

2017-18 Homes SOLD for Original ARV Appraisal or Higher

Cherwenka Realty Team RESULTS-100%

"They said we would never sell homes in these areas for these prices"

479 Park Valley Drive NW; Atlanta 30318-**UNDER CONTRACT $219,800**-Original ARV $180,000

1157 Oakland drive SW; Atlanta 30310-**UNDER CONTRACT $259,800**-Original ARV $210,000

240 West Lake Drive NW; Atlanta 30314-**UNDER CONTRACT $199,800**-Original ARV $160,000

106 Chappell Road NW; Atlanta 30314-**UNDER CONTRACT $219,800**-Original $200,000

2467 Harvell Drive NW; Atlanta 30318-**SOLD $175,500**-Original ARV $160,000

234 Florida Ave SW; Atlanta 30310-**SOLD $209,800**-Original ARV $180,000

1888 La Mesa Lane; Decatur 30332-**UNDER CONTRACT $189,800**-Original ARV $160,000

8 S. Eugenia Place; Atlanta 30318-**SOLD $259,800**-Original ARV $200,000

588 Hamilton E Holmes Drive; Atlanta 30318-**SOLD $179,800**-Original ARV $160,000

919 Coleman Street SE; Atlanta 30315-**SOLD $179,800**-Original ARV $160,000

1690 Lanier Drive SW; Atlanta-**SOLD $199,800**-Original ARV $160,000

3010 Waters Road SE; Atlanta- **UNDER CONTRACT $249,500**-Original ARV $180,000

5 Gertrude Place; Atlanta 30318-**UNDER CONTRACT $299,800**-Original ARV $200,000

3 Gertrude Place; Atlanta 30318-**SOLD $259,800**-Original ARV $220,000

1685 Donald Lee Hollowell Blvd; Atlanta 30318-**SOLD $205,000**-Original ARV $180,000

533 Park Valley Dr; Atlanta 30318-**SOLD $199,800**-Original ARV $160,000

2216 Baker Road; Atlanta 30318-**SOLD $159,800**-Original ARV $140,000

20 Holly Road; Atlanta 30314-**SOLD $169,800**-Original ARV $160,000

2012 Joseph E. Boone Blvd; Atlanta 30314-**SOLD $169,800**-Original ARV $160,000

246 Florida Ave SW; Atlanta 30311-**SOLD $219,800**-Original ARV $195,000

2351 Cross Street NW; Atlanta 30318-**SOLD $179,800**-Original ARV $150,000

1680 Hadlock Street SW; Atlanta 30311-**SOLD $169,800**-Original Arv $140,000

670 Indigo Lane NW; Atlanta 30318-**SOLD $179,800**-Original ARV $160,000

1675 Brewer Blvd SW; Atlanta 30310-**SOLD $179,800**-Original ARV $160,000

365 Adelle Street SE; Atlanta 30315-**SOLD $159,800**-Original ARV $150,000

354 Adelle Street SE; Atlanta 30315-**SOLD $159,800**-Original ARV $150,000

2058 Chicago Ave NW; Atlanta 30314-**SOLD $159,800**-Original ARV $150,000

2475 Harvel Drive NW; Atlanta 30318-**SOLD $168,000**-Original ARV $160,000

1490 W. Austin Road; Decatur 30032-**SOLD $195,000**-Original ARV $150,000

1150 Wyland Drive SW; Atlanta 30310-**SOLD $179,800**-Original ARV $140,000

1078 Ashby Grove SW; Atlanta 30314-**SOLD $199,800**-Original ARV $165,000

1003 Parson St SW; Atlanta 30314-**SOLD $219,800**-Original $180,000

1468 Westridge Road SW; Atlanta 30310-**SOLD $169,800**-Original ARV $140,000

1594 Alder Lane SW; Atlanta 30310-**SOLD $179,800**-Original ARV $160,000

2881 Oldknow Drive NW; Atlanta 30318-**SOLD $159,800**-Original ARV $120,000

256 Judy Lane SW; Atlanta 30315-**UNDER CONTRACT $159,800**-Original ARV $150,000

741 Cascade Ave SW; Atlanta 30310-**SOLD $179,800**-Original ARV $180,000

1790 Brewer Blvd SW; Atlanta 30311-**SOLD $179,800**-Original ARV $150,000

1008 Parsons Street NW; Atlanta 30314-**SOLD $159,800**-Original ARV $150,000

1142 Westmont Road SW; Atlanta 30310-**SOLD $149,800**-Original ARV $140,000

1816 Avon Ave SW; Atlanta 30311-**SOLD $179,800**-Original ARV $150,000

1358 Dennis Drive; Decatur 30032-**SOLD $155,000**-Original ARV $130,000

2970 Wanda Circle SW; Atlanta 30315-**SOLD $193,000**-Original ARV $150,000

1594 Beecher Street SW; Atlanta 30310-**SOLD $179,800**-Original ARV $150,000

885 Thurmond Street NW; Atlanta 30314-**SOLD $159,800**-Original ARV $130,000

2407 Antwerp Drive SW; Atlanta 30315-**SOLD $132,000**-Original ARV $130,000

2960 1st Ave SW; Atlanta 30315-**SOLD $129,800**-Original ARV $125,000

2834 Lynda Place; Decatur 30032-**SOLD $150,000**-Original ARV $140,000

2512 Campbellton Road SW; Atlanta 30311-**SOLD $139,700**-Original ARV 130,000

2130 Green Forrest Drive; Decatur 30032-**SOLD $130,000**-Original ARV $130,000

1050 Hugo St SW; Atlanta 30315-**SOLD $160,000**-Original ARV $130,000

3217 Hammerskjold Drive; East Point-**SOLD $132,000**-Original ARV $130,000

1645 Alverado Terrace SW; Atlanta 30310-**SOLD $155,200**-Original ARV $150,000

1120 Cahaba Drive SW; Atlanta 30310-**SOLD $130,000**-Original ARV $130,000

316 Dargan Place SW; Atlanta 30314-**SOLD $190,000**-Original ARV $160,000

2702 Aquamist Drive; Decatur 30034-**SOLD $150,000-**Original ARV $140,000

1606 Hollyhock Drive; Decatur 30032-**SOLD $159,700-**Original ARV $150,000

4099 Snapfinger Way; Decatur 30034-**SOLD $127,500-**Original ARV $120,000

1950 La Mesa Lane; Decatur 30032-**SOLD $151,000-**Original ARV $140,000

1693 Derrill Drive; Decatur 30032-**SOLD $155,000-**Original ARV $130,000

1762 Timothy Drive SW; Atlanta 30311-**SOLD $133,000-**Original ARV $130,000

1842 Lakewood Terrace SW; Atlanta 30315-**SOLD $156,500-**Original ARV $160,000

1567 Willow Brook Lane; Decatur 30032-**SOLD $129,700-**Original ARV $130,000

1877 Windsor Drive SW; Atlanta 30311-**SOLD $138,000-**Original ARV $130,000

2982 McAfee Road; Decatur 30032-**SOLD $136,500-**Original ARV $135,000

1046 Orlando Place SW; Atlanta 30310-**SOLD $139,700-**Original ARV $140,000

CHAPTER 15

A Day in the Life of the Most Successful Skin-In Wholesaler

Risk it; go for it. Life always gives you another chance, another go at it. It's very important to take enormous risks.

—Mary Quant

Skin-In Wholesaler Explained

Our role as real estate wholesalers is similar to flipping except that the time frame is much shorter and no repairs are made to the home before the wholesaler sells it. A real estate wholesaler contracts with a home seller and markets the home to his or her buyers. The wholesaler makes a profit, which is the difference between the contracted price with the seller and the amount paid by the buyer.

Why are we different from all others? I don't assign contracts. Most wholesalers assign the contract and use other people's money in the transaction. In our experience, we have learned that those wholesalers *do not* make the decisions that are best for their client. We close on a house even if we don't have a buyer. We buy houses with the intentions of remodeling them ourselves. When you're a skin-in wholesaler, you're not going to buy a house that doesn't truly meet the after-repair-value requirements.

The question we get, postrecession, is how are you flipping more than one hundred per year after that brutal recession? Instead of us continuing to answer the question, we documented the steps you must take to help you reach your economic goals.

Most wholesalers will describe their role the way we define a bird dog, a person who assigns and doesn't close on a property. Because of the significant disadvantages of the bird dog role that we listed in the bird dog section on this book, it's more lucrative for us be skin-in wholesalers, people who negotiate with the seller and who use their own funds for earnest money and closing fees and who close on the property—typically within seven days.

Without further ado, let's address the number-one question that we receive. Mike has flipped more than 2,100 hundred properties since 1996. And he has flipped more than one hundred a year since 2011. How does he do it?

TOP SECRET

Skin-In Wholesaler Truly Controls the Property via the Purchase and Sale Agreement

After listening to the newbies and so-called advanced investors spend their days looking for their deals, we learned that most people waste time. Let's discuss what doesn't work first:

TOP SECRET

• Knock Knock—Who's Not There. You can motivate a seller to sell his or her home. There are unsuccessful skin-in wholesalers who go door to door in their target area to smoke out sellers. I am sure we can find a rare story where that methods work, but in most instances, it's a complete waste of time.

- Scratch My Back and I'll Scratch Yours. Investors offer $500–$1,000 fees for referrals and wonder why they don't get a single call. It's because no one believes you. If they believe you, they don't want to wait until you close (when we have titles issues, a deal could take months or years to close).
- Bandit Signs. The real estate courses that tell you to place bandit signs on street corners are asking you to commit a criminal offense. Code enforcement will come after you sooner or later. You will lose money paying fines if you go down this path. The best route is to place the sign on a property.

Now that we know what doesn't work, we are going to cover the methods Mike used to start his skin-in wholesale deal. Twenty-one years ago, Mike hired a husband-and-wife team to work as a deal tracker (day laborer) and his admin (hourly), respectively. Mike trained them on his buying criteria in his target area.

His deal tracker left every day with the streets he was covering highlighted on a map. As you may recall, earlier in the book we said that you must create a goal list. This is an example of how to apply what you planned. In this instance, Mike determined what streets would be the next big thing. Then he executed on his plan to get distressed houses in his target areas.

The deal tracker searched based on Mike's *buy* criteria:

- Distressed homes that need thousands of dollars in repairs. All bargains are worth analyzing, no matter what shape the house is in. If the house is extremely ugly, that gives you the opportunity to buy it for a bargain price.
- Most of the homes we buy are abandoned, but it's not a requirement. Additionally, we purchase short sales.
- If it has disgusting carpet that makes you lose your lunch, pull up a corner of the carpet, without damaging it, to see if there are hardwoods underneath.
- As-is condition is expected.

- Electrical shot? Who cares? It's best to rewire in most instances.
- No heating and air system? Who cares? We replace air systems the majority of the time.
- If it's under my square-foot requirement, it's not a deal killer. We determine if an addition makes sense. [Note: since we work in the South, people are accustomed to space, so anything that's the size of an apartment is hard to sell.]

What Mike Called His "Deal (Seller) Tracker Responsibilities"

The deal tracker was responsible for bringing Mike the address and a photo of a vacant house or abandoned house he found. This arrangement worked because Mike would pay him at the end of the day. Pay for the deal tracker based on his or her experience rate ranged from $50–$100 per day for each address and photo of a vacant and abandoned home.

Mike's guy worked every day for years, but you can hire someone to work part-time. Perhaps, that's a job you can give a family member.

Admin and the Bag of Goodies

Mike's admin sent letters to the sellers offering to purchase their home. Mike kept the deal-tracker role for around for years to obtain off-market properties. Then he evolved into this model to support the demand from buyers.

- Priced well below ARV
- Our target for properties to receive the highest and fastest ROI
- Vacant for quick flip
- Institutionally owned for clear title
- Need considerable rehab for the greatest discounts
- Low foot traffic

Where Do Mike and Tolla Find Their Houses!

Agents, agents, and more agents—Mike and Tolla network with agents to get the pocket listings. These are properties that are technically for sale, but agents and buyers won't find them listed on the multiple listing service, the database they use to peruse local options for clients. Likewise, home buyers won't find pocket listings online or by a For Sale sign in the front yard, either. Instead, the real estate agent who's been hired for a pocket listing keeps it in his metaphorical pocket (along with photos possibly) and shares it only with a smattering of buyers he knows and who he trusts can turn him on to the right clientele. Agents bring these pocket listings because he performs, puts it under contract, and closes. There are lots of people out there who don't. Other sources for bargain houses are the following:

- Multiple listing service, banks, and REOS
- Courthouse
- GoldminePropeties.net—Distressed sellers fill out the form on my site.
- Bird dogs
- Social media
- Craig's List
- Title company

How Does Mike Attract Buyers?

Step 1 Create the Package

After Mike secured the contract with earnest money, his team would create detailed repair estimates. (Have a general contractor walk the property with you to get the repair estimate.) Then Mike created a marketing package for the property that contained the following:

- A property flyer that explains the ARV (see next page to see one of our flyers)
- Property photos
- Certified appraisal
- Detailed contractor estimate

Step 2 Market the Wholesale Deal

Over the years, we have perfected focusing on the marketing strategies that work in today's market. We use the following tools to sell our wholesale deals in twenty-four hours or less:

- Constant contact
- GoldmineProperties.net
- Craigslist.com
- Facebook.com
- Text-alert service

The most effective methods are also the simplest. The greatest component of social media is that others advertise for you by sharing your deals. Social media has helped us create a database of hungry buyers.

TOP SECRET

If you're a newbie, continue to advertise your property after it goes under contract to continue to build your buyer database.

Due Diligence

When the buyer expresses interest in our property, we do not allow him or her to have due diligence time. If they're going to inspect, it must be done before their contract is binding. We don't negotiate. Price is the same for everyone because my deals are priced to sell. That's why we get the appraisal to take the subjectivity value. Mike's wholesale fee is five thousand dollars unless we make improvements to the property.

When the buyer sends the full price offer with the nonrefundable twenty-five hundred dollars in earnest money, we place the property under contract on goldminepropties.net website. This lets our buyer know that our deals go fast Mike requires twenty-five hundred dollars to reduce the risk of the buyer back out.

CHAPTER 16

Making Money with Buy-and-Hold

Landlords make money in their sleep.

—John Stuart Mill

In Chicago, Mike's father made millions in real estate working full-time as an agent and landlord of many multiunit buildings. Tolla's father acquired real estate as he traveled the United States in the army. At the peak of Mike's investment portfolio, he owned ninety-three Section 8 properties that brought in large, on-time deposits. Tolla turned her personal home into a rental property. Buy-and-hold investing is one of the ways that we have created long-term wealth. In this chapter, we will discuss the advantages and disadvantages of keeping some of the properties you fix in the portfolio.

Advantages

Capital Appreciation

Capital appreciation is a rise in the value of the investment property based on a rise in market value. In real estate, this occurs when the property investment commands a higher price in the market than you originally paid for the property. Profits are higher when investors maximize deductions and reduce operating expenses.

Your Tenant Pays the Mortgage

Therefore, the longer you hold the property, the more of the loan principal your tenants are paying down and the more wealth you are creating for yourself. Every year that you hold the property, you are using the tenant's money to pay off your debt. You can access the money by selling or refinancing.

Tax Write-Off

You can write-off interest on the mortgage or on any credit cards used to make purchases if you buy and hold property. Moreover, you can write-off your insurance, home office, repairs, travel expenses, any legal and professional fees, and property taxes. Go to Nolo.com for a more extensive list. Additionally, the government allows you to depreciate the purchase price of your property based on a set depreciation schedule, even if your property is actually appreciating in value.

Monthly Income

You will have cash each month that you did not have to work for that your property produces for you.

Leverage

Rental properties can be purchased with borrowed funds. This means that you can purchase a rental property by putting down only a percentage of the total value.

Disadvantages

It's true that you may have headaches with tenants, repairs, and devoting time, even if you have a property manager.

You will be in the business of owning real estate, so you will need to run it like a business enterprise. There are tools available to help you run your rental enterprise effectively.

- You can set up online payments to receive payments promptly.
- Hire traditional or use virtual assistant and property management services like www.davincivirtual.com.
- Respect your tenant's right to "quiet enjoyment" but arrange in the lease agreement to inspect the property yearly.
- Use a clear tenant agreement that spells your expectations out and verbally explains those expectations to each tenant.

Owning rental property is a wise investment to your portfolio, whether you're investing in single residences or multifamily. You have to make the commitment to set your rental enterprise up for success.

FINAL CHAPTER

Put Your Big Boy or Girl Panties On and Build Generational Wealth

You can't start the final chapter if you keep rereading the last.

—Anonymous

Stop procrastinating and start listening to your heart; it's telling you to leap. Chase your dreams. You don't need to punch the clock and hate Monday because you're worried about bills or you're wondering how long the real estate boom will last. Have the courage to go out of your comfort zone If you tried before but experienced many failures, don't lose faith because the fruits of your labor will bloom. Rehabbing won't be easy, but it's going to be worth it. Don't listen to people who have not been to where you are trying to get to. Trust your plan. You don't need to be perfect, you don't need to be the best, and you don't need to be an expert. You have to have courage and action. You live your own life. As you traverse through life's journey ten or twenty years from now, don' t create a road interweaved with a what-if. Create a new action plan each day. Since great results are about great action, we are going to leave you with these powerful action quotes.

1. "Do you want to know who you are? Don't ask. Act! Action will delineate and define you" (Thomas Jefferson).
2. "Small deeds done are better than great deeds planned")Peter Marshall).
3. "Action is the foundational key to all success" (Pablo Picasso).
4. "The path to success is to take massive, determined actions" (Tony Robbins).

5. "You don't have to be great to start, but you have to start to be great" (Zig Ziglar).

After reading this book, you have all the information you need to be successful in starting or growing your flipping business. You can do anything you put your mind to. You just have to be willing to work for it.

God bless and Godspeed!

THE GODFATHER'S COMPLETE TESTIMONY

Stripped Bare by the Lord, Part One

Train a child in the way he should go, and when he is old
he will not turn from it. (Proverbs 22:6)

How grateful I am that my mother was a beautiful Christian woman
who brought our family to church and taught us how to live righteously
for the Lord. If it wasn't for my mother's prayers, and the prayers of those
she fellowshipped with, I might still be a forever lost sinner who deserved
God's severe judgment.

So here is my story of college and the corporate world, ten years in the
male dance revue business, being born again—October 8, 1995, making a
career change into real estate, losing everything we had, and accumulating
$100,000 of debt, my turnaround in real estate, and the dozens of times
God's divine intervention kept my hope alive and made my faith in him
even stronger.

My senior year in college, several girls at school dared me to enter a
local male strip contest where the winner won five hundred dollars. Hey,
in college that's a lot of money, especially when you're eating macaroni
and cheese as your daily diet! I won, and Jerry Thornton, the owner of
a local male revue, asked me to join his group. We averaged three shows
a week and were paid $100 per show, plus another $100 or so in tips. I
was having fun, and the attention from the girls was really cool. This was
also a big stress reliever after competing in athletics throughout college
and just finishing my last national competition in springboard diving. I
was fortunate to have my school paid for on an athletic scholarship, win
nationals on three-meter, and achieve all-American honors four times—
not to mention the long hours of always having to study and study and

study. I would graduate with a marketing degree in May 1986 from Wright State University in Dayton, Ohio.

1983 Three-Meter National Champion

After graduation, I needed a break and did not want to interview for the corporate world until fall. After all, this dancing stuff was new and exciting. My parents did not favor the idea of me taking my clothes off (only to a G-string) for a living.

That summer was great. I had the opportunity to weight train every day and add twenty pounds to my once-162-pound diving physique and grow my hair. I started a strip-o-gram business called "First-Class Strippers," you know, the stripper dressed as a cop going to a bachelorette party making a noise or parking citation, turning on the boom box and doing his duty. Along with doing three to four shows with Hunk-A-Mania male dance revue, I was now making $1,500 plus a week.

Fall came too soon, and my parents were expecting me to get a J-O-B, job. I honored my word and took a position with Dunn and Bradstreet Credit Services as a sales representative, making $34,000 base salary plus 8 percent commissions, which was a good job coming out of college in 1986. Wearing a suit and making sales presentations made me feel like a business professional.

The corporate world provided a good business foundation for me learning real-life sales training techniques you don't learn in college; it prepared me to take second in a four-month regional sales contest. After eighteen months, I became disenchanted with the political correctness and brownnosing that goes on in the office environment, and I resigned.

I teamed up with Tommy Thompson, aka "Solid Gold," one of the most popular and successful male dancers in America, and we put our own show together. The strip-o-gram business was booming at seventy-five dollars a shot for ten minutes of work.

As the show became more successful, our tours expanded regionally and nationally. The Phil Donahue Show called February 1990 and wanted to do a special on our male dance revue. After the interviews, they were more interested in a story about, me, aka "Malibu Ken." The rest of the guys felt betrayed that they were not going to be on the show, although I had a say on Phil Donahue's decision. Their revenge was to split from me, and when we came home from taping the show, I had no male revue. Can you say "huge adversity!" I was fortunate to recruit four strong entertainers out of Columbus, Ohio, rehearse for a week, book shows, and change the name to Mike "Malibu" Mills (Cherwenka didn't cut it for a last name) and the American Hunks. I wore the hats of booking agent, MC, and feature entertainer, and took part in some of the choreography. I took the show from a local level to international within a year.

After the Donahue show aired, our lives began to change. It was one of the highest rated shows in daytime TV at the time, which lead to more television exposure—three appearances on *The Jerry Springer Show*, the first show of HBO's *Real Sex*, Joan Rivers's show, Montel Williams's show, the Good Company Show, *Evening Magazine*, *Playgirl* magazine, *Daily Star Enquire*, and two more appearances on *The Phil Donahue Show*, which included "The Best of Phil Donahue" and his twenty-fifth anniversary. With success comes jealousy. Solid Gold turned us in to the Mattel Toy Company for using the names Malibu Ken and Barbie. The company sued because we had acts resembling the dolls coming to life in one of our routines. This actually gave us even more exposure, as we were on the front page of tabloids and in the news.

Life was grand! We were recognized by the public nearly everywhere we went, and we had all the worldly stuff, friends, possessions, new home, success, and pleasure. Then events started to change. On December 3, 1993, I was blessed with a beautiful baby girl we named Tiffany. Becoming a father, I then took on new responsibilities, and my outlook on life changed. I was not the model father you read about in parenting magazines. My schedule consisted of being out of town three out of four weeks of the month, and when I was home, I spent ten hours a day in the office booking shows. I provided well for my family, but that's about it. What I did for a living was a business, and the fame and attention had no significance anymore. I started feeling a serious void in my life, an empty feeling deep within. I wish I had a quarter every time someone had asked me, "How long you are going to dance?" My response was, "What else am I going to do? I'm making a decent six-figure income that supports our lifestyle."

On March 30, 1995, we moved to a nice home in Atlanta from Dayton, Ohio, because most of my work was in the southeast, and we liked the more temperate climate and the opportunities of a larger city. Tom Gill was the most loyal and talented person I ever had work for me, and he gave his life to Christ in 1993. Tom has the gift of evangelism and made every effort to convert me. When Tom came to Atlanta in July 1995 to visit, I knew he was going to witness to me hard and heavy. I was not ready to throw both legs over the fence and change, so I gave God lip service when saying the sinner's prayer just to pacify Tom. God did not find that funny, so he put a storm in my life to get my attention. According to Hebrews 12:5–6, when the Lord punishes you, don't make light of it, and when he corrects you, don't be discouraged. The Lord corrects the people he loves and disciplines those he calls his own. The show started to lack in quality, the guys were fighting among each other, my '34 RV blew two engines, the girls' van was stolen, I was on tour in Nova Scotia, Canada, and my wife wanted a divorce, and so on. Times were getting so bad that God put the writing on the wall: "Either you give your life to me, or I am going to take it."

My next tour was in Oklahoma; Tom Gill encouraged me to see Don Schwartz, who was also an outstanding entertainer and recently a born-again Christian. Don had worked for me when I was with Solid Gold and now lived in Houston, Texas. I had Sunday and Monday off, and I flew in to see Don. At this time, I knew the reason I felt so empty was because I was separated from a relationship with my creator, my Lord and Savior Jesus Christ. I felt dirty, unclean, and I was living in sin. On Sunday, October 8, 1995, I trusted Christ with my eternity; I confessed that I was a lost sinner, asked for forgiveness, and thanked God for sending his son to die for my sin debt. "For all have sinned and fall short of the glory of God" (Romans 3:23). I wanted my life to now glorify my heavenly father. I wept like a child that night as the Holy Spirit filled me with joy, peace, and happiness. I was a new creation.

> Therefore, if anyone is in Christ, he is a new creation; the
> old has gone, the new has come. (1 Corinthians 5:17)

Through faith in Jesus, each one of us can be forgiven and restored to have fellowship with our maker. Through the blood Jesus shed on the cross, that feeling of emptiness I once had has been replaced by the assurance of peace and hope for the future.

Our next show was Tuesday, and I told my guys about my salvation and that there would be no more American Hunks after Christmas. They, along with others in the industry, thought I'd lost my mind. Why would Mike "Malibu" Mills and the American Hunks, the most successful male dance revue in the country next to Chippendales, give it all away? My faith was immediately tested that night as we had a huge sold-out show and the guys got drunk and challenged some of my decisions. For the first time, I felt naked on stage and had no desire to entertain.

As my contractual obligations were coming to an end, I must admit I had fears about where my next dollar was going to come from. As I drove home from our last show in December 1995, I had thought of keeping one costume and tape just in case I had to perform in an emergency financial situation. Driving thirty-five miles an hour one block from where I'd parked the RV, the new engine blew up. I believe that was God intervening, telling me that I'd best sell out and trust in him totally. "Trust in the Lord with all your heart and lean not on your own understanding; in all your ways acknowledge him, and he will make your paths straight" (Proverbs 3:5–6). Within two weeks I sold my show to a competitor from Birmingham, Alabama, and kept nothing.

End of story? Hardly, it's just the beginning. As a newborn Christian, I was on fire for Jesus and just wanted to share my salvation with others, read God's word, fellowship with other believers, and be the best husband and father I could be. Oh, yeah, I still didn't have a job or know what I was going to do for a living. I think they call it *walking in faith*. I had a great support group of Christian brothers. Donnie Hoover was the pastor to receive me as I walked down the aisle at Charles Stanley's First Baptist Atlanta, Tim Gunter was the pastor at our Wednesday morning Bible study, Tom Gill and Don Schwartz (both have full-time ministries) gave me weekly support, and of course, my mom and dad had their whole church praying for us.

Tiffany was playing with the Sunday paper, and as I was cleaning up, a foreclosure seminar advertisement caught my attention. What better way to supplement a six-digit income than real estate! So I went to the seminar and bought all the books and tapes, joined the Georgia Real Estate Investors Association, went to more seminars, and bought even more books and tapes.

On April 15, 1996, I bought my first foreclosure property, and the following month, I purchased two more. Well, anything that could go wrong did. The wholesaler that sold me the properties committed fraud, cheated by the contractors, and every time I had a property under contract, it fell through.

It was now December 1996, and if it had cost fifty cents to travel around the world, I couldn't have afforded to get out of sight. God had completely broken me. I hadn't made a dime in twelve months, and I was in grossly huge debt and crying out to God for answers. My mind-set was "How I can share my testimony with anyone?" I'd thought God would bless me economically since I'd given up a lucrative career and just walked out in faith; instead, I was sleeping over at the properties I was fixing up, with no utilities and taking my showers at the truck stop. I was working fourteen hours hard labor each day and waiting for another credit card application to come in the mail so I could get through another month. My parents would not loan me any more money.

I went to see my pastor, Dr. Frank Cox, at North Metro First Baptist Church. One of my big hang-ups before giving my life to Christ was whether God still intervened in the twenty-first century. Sure, I believed in all the Old Testament stories, but I wanted to be certain God was going to take care of my family during a career change. After pouring my heart out to Dr. Frank and expecting him to encourage me with scripture or a testimony of someone in a similar situation, his response was "How much do you need?" My heart fell to the floor, thinking $100,000 grand would do for now, but your cheap pockets might spare $100. No, thanks. There was never any thought of asking for a nickel. *I needed a miracle!*

On Sunday, December 15, I felt called to cut my hair that was past my shoulders. That was the only thing I'd held on to from past, because others told me the look would open doors to share my testimony. The next day I was working at the property and listening to Dr. Charles Stanley on the radio, and I just broke down and lost it. Screaming, crying and kicking boxes, I was angry at God, asking him to give me a sign that it was going to be all right or just take my life. I couldn't take it anymore; I was doing everything possible to make it work, and nothing was. This was not the deal I'd asked for. Some of the scriptures I meditated on were the following: "Without faith it is impossible to please God, because anyone who comes to him must believe that he exists and that he rewards those who earnestly seek him" (Hebrew 11:6) and "I am the vine, you are the branches. If a man remains in me and me in him, he will bear much fruit; apart from me you can do nothing" (John 15:5).

Where was my fruit? Where were my rewards? Why were my family and I going through this pain? We are living righteously, God-fearing Christians, and we tithed one hundred dollars a week because we needed to make fifty thousand dollars to pay bills. The story of Job related well. Suffering is part of the human experience, and Job is a valuable resource to turn to when suffering overwhelms us. God is in control over all things and is worthy of our worship, even though we may not understand what he is doing in our lives.

One Tuesday morning, I woke up after sleeping at the property, and two huge trees on the side of the house where I needed to put a driveway had been split in half by lightning (see pictures below), and there was no other storm damage in the county! Neither tree had fallen on the two houses I'd been working on, nor did I hear a noise in my sleep. My spirits were restored, and God's greatness was in my presence.

The next day at Wednesday's Bible study, Jim Patrick loaned me $15,000 to finish repairs on the last house. Earlier in the month, Jim had said he did not feel comfortable with the loan. I was able to purchase a few things for my family the following Wednesday for Christmas after all. Sold the first house January 31, 1997, and the other two in March. Repairs were more than double the original estimates, so we lost considerable money.

GOD. TALKIN

By April 1, we were $100,000 in debt and thirty days from bankruptcy, and this is no April Fool's joke. My sister Doris sent me a scripture for inspiration: "For I know the plans I have for you, declares the LORD, plans to prosper you and not to harm you, plans to give you hope and a future" (Jeremiah 29:11). I meditated on that verse with all my heart and soul. I knew the only way to get out of debt and to get food on the table quickly was to wholesale some real estate. Although retailing allows for much larger profits, it also is a several-months-long process. The LORD allowed me to put a property under contract, borrow the $500 earnest money, do a simultaneous closing between the buyer and seller, and net $6,000 without owning the property for five minutes. That was my first wholesale deal. God was with me as we did sixty-nine wholesale deals in 1997 (paid off all our debt) and over one hundred a year since then, acquired ninety-three rental properties, and blessed us with more economic success than we had ever imagined. Greatness in Jesus Christ.

I credit real estate guru John Adams for launching my career

God has allowed my wholesaling business to be my ministry. He gives me the ability to find these great deals and help others prosper financially. What a blessing to help others for a living and share the lessons from the challenges I went through.

If God is the all-consuming, all-powerful, all-knowing, loving and infinite creator, sustainer, and redeemer of this universe, then nothing else matters quite as much as getting to know him—and to know him well!

Gravedigger Ministries Fundraiser
With Ex-Governor Barnes
April 2006

As I mentioned before, one of my hang-ups before putting my faith and trust in Jesus Christ was the uncertainty of the kind of divine relationship expected. The following are events where God has intervened:

- August 1984. The summer before my sophomore year in college, I was driving back to Fort Pierce, Florida, from Austin, Texas, after training at the university that summer. I ran out of gas at about the halfway point, with no more money to my name. After spending the night sleeping on top of my Datsun 280 ZX in a church parking lot, I realized the only hope of financial help was the church to get me back to Indian River Junior College where I was attending school. I told the pastor my situation and assured him the debt would be paid back within seventy-two hours. His response was, "I will give you half of what you need, and God will provide the rest." I said to myself, "You have to be kidding. How cheap can you get?" Well, as I was nearing empty on my gas tank again, I picked up a hitchhiker, and he had money— well, at least more than I had. He put me up for the night at his mother's house in Gainesville, Florida, provided a good breakfast and gave me enough money to get home. This experience provided a foundation of faith and a reference to fall back on that God did provide when needed.

- • January 1996–January 1997. During the first thirteen months of my career change, while having no income, I somehow always paid my bills and salvaged my credit, which is imperative for real estate success. Many people loaned me money, and I filled out every credit application I could get my hands on. I was debt free by Christmas 1997 and had my first million net worth by Christmas 1998. I can't tell you how many times it seemed like a deal was not going to close and it did, or how when every nickel from a sale was spoken for, I was able to pay off a debt at the last minute right before the due date. I was on my knees so much in prayer, a pair of knee pads would have helped. God was faithful.

- September 18, 1996. I was off to the pawn shop to hawk about $10,000 worth of jewelry from my dancing days; I used to look like Mr. T, with a ring on every finger and a half-dozen necklaces. I was driving our last vehicle, a 1979 Ford van. We'd sold the Corvette convertible the previous month to survive. Long story short, I avoided a deadly accident. God saying everything is all right when at the moment it seemed disastrous.

- October 12, 1996. I was building a carport at my rehab property, and I was on the roof installing four-by-eight plywood sheets for decking when the whole carport fell down with me on top. I was able to jump far enough out without having all that lumber on top of me. Could have lost my life or been paralyzed but only sprained my ankle: God telling me life is a gift and *he* can take it at any time.

- January 19, 1997. A couple in our Bible study both lost their jobs and gave their testimony on how God took care of them: great encouragement at the time.

- January 21, 1997. I burned the woods down on the Stonewall Tell Road property (the same house as the carport incident). My brother-in-law needed work, so I gave him some painting to do. The work was not completed on deadline, and I spoke harshly to him (certainly not Christ-like). I went to the back of the house where we burned trash, put a little too much gasoline on the debris, the wind picked up, and before you knew it, an acre of woods was on fire. The fire station was a mile down the street, and they took care of putting out the flame along with tearing up the yard. God was telling me to keep my cool to avoid the heat.

- September 15, 1998. Our second child, Michael, was born. Life was wonderful but definitely not taking anything for granted! November 8, 1988, baby Michael was on the bed, and I was on my knees next to the bed playing with him. The thought that came to mind was, Why don't I pray on my knees anymore as I used to? Baby Michael started choking and stopped breathing. Can you imagine the fear at this time? I called 911, and while waiting for the paramedics, I prayed to God for help and promised I would be back in prayer on my knees. This was God saying, "Don't get too comfortable."

- July 9, 1998. A couple of examples where God is protecting our children. Tiffany, five years older than Michael, was in my office after I'd installed some bookshelves. She was playing underneath the shelves for thirty minutes, and just after she moved, the bookshelves collapsed. Tiffany would have been badly hurt, had she still been under them. November 2, 1998. Again, Tiffany was in the office on the chair, and she fell off, just missing the pointed edge of the desk by an inch. She would have split her head open. September 16, 1998. Michael was on the landing area upstairs, holding onto the railing when he decided to let go and sat down right at the edge of the top of the flight of stairs. One more inch further, and he would have fallen down a big flight of stairs and been badly hurt.

- December 9, 1999. Talking to an investor on Hill Street between our cars, which are three feet apart, a stolen car ran out of control down the street about fifty miles an hour and hit the back of my car, which rammed into the back of the investor's car. I jumped out of the way, the bumper hit my thigh, and I couldn't walk for a week. A second later, both of my legs would have been crushed between the two cars. Not to mention the thugs pointed a gun in my face as they jumped out of their stolen car to flee from danger. How many lives is God going to give me?

Stripped Bare by the Lord, Part 2

Divorce, Real Estate Collapse, and Remarried

I am the vine; you are the branches. If a man remains in me and me in him, he will bear much fruit: apart from me you can do nothing. (John 15:5)

Postdivorce

On August 31, 2004, I was served with divorce papers. I felt blessed, relieved, happy, and renewed, and did I say happy? A fresh start in life! We should have divorced years prior, but my religious convictions would not let me pull the trigger, so the way it all unfolded was perfect—except the part about the $5,000 monthly alimony, insurance, most of the furniture, and a big lump-sum cash payment. It didn't matter. God has given me a clean, free, and happy soul. You can't put a price tag on that.

How I Met My African American Wife, Tolla Soto

Houses and riches are an inheritance from fathers. But a prudent wife is from the Lord. (Proverbs 19:14)

He who finds a wife finds a good thing and obtains favor from the Lord. (Proverbs 18:22)

Proverbs 31:10–31—"The Wife of Noble Character"

Yes, I am truly blessed. God has given me a gorgeous wife I truly love and respect.

Tolla and I married November 16, 2013, so let me backtrack since there is some history to fill in. I coached the 2003 five-to-six-year-old coed basketball team at Dacula Park, and Tolla's daughter, Lauren, and my son, Michael, were both on the same team. Well, my first reaction was, *All right, I have a hot mom on my team,* and then I find out Tolla lived two doors down from me with another man. They were the only black couple in our subdivision.

So Tolla was there to witness my last year of marriage and my ex-wife's character. We became friends during the basketball season and social events at our homes. After the divorce, Tolla became a very good, trusted friend. She helped me refurnish my home (which took a lot of time, effort, and expertise), plan my Goldmine Properties Christmas parties, clothes shop for the children. (can you picture an attractive interracial couple shopping at the Mall of Georgia in Gwinnett County in 2004 with the kids? It would have been nice to get a dollar for every look and ten dollars for every ten-second stare.)

You are probably asking why we didn't start dating back then? A couple of reasons:

1. Tolla was in a relationship and living with another man, and I would never cross that line.

2. I was in a relationship, and my type has always been five six to five eight, long, blond hair, blue eyes, and large breasts. Well, let's just say I got teased for dating the Barbie type.

Tolla has witnessed a pretty entertaining dating landscape and was a helpful advisor. We both admit now that we have thought about what it would have been like to have dated back then.

You can't have love without respect. And Tolla was the most successful and hardest-working businesswoman I knew, which made me stand up and pay attention. Nothing is more attractive than being able to discuss business ideas with a woman! She ran multiple businesses (largest hair salon in DeKalb County, a technology consulting firm, real estate agent, and I helped her and her then-partner get started in the building business). Can you say drive and motivation?

As the market started to take a turn in 2006, so did Tolla's businesses and relationship. She moved out of her home December 2006, and we did not reconnect until December 2012. I don't know about you, but anyone heavily invested in real estate during the bust got hurt badly. We both lost nearly everything. I will talk about those disturbing emotions and how it took my faith to the next level. The years 2007 to 2014 were some very dark times.

Tolla reached out to me November 2012 via Facebook about a charity event she was having and asked if I wanted to donate any clothes. I took her up on it, cleaned out my well overdue closet (did the PMA thing and left half the closet empty for my next wife to put her clothes) and brought over enough clothes to open a store. She invited me to dinner, and then we danced at Johnny's Hideaway. We kissed in the parking lot and had that aha moment. God had planted a seed of trust, respect, and attraction for each other that evening. There is so much comfort when you know you can trust someone.

Oh yeah, one little problem: I was in a six-month relationship that was good. Hurting someone's feeling was not my style, and getting out of this relationship wasn't easy. While I sorted out my feelings, Tolla hung out platonically. I was completely honest with Tolla about this, and I thank her to this day for hanging in there. It is safe to say these events strengthened our relationship.

Tolla lived in Inman Park and I in Dacula, so every Thursday we had date night. The kids called it "Secret Thursday" because they would be shipped off to a friend's house and didn't know why. I often spent the night, as the drive home was forty-five minutes. On May 18, 2013, I proposed marriage to Tolla, and she accepted. On November 16, 2013, we married. At the wedding, Tolla's Dad came up to me and thanked me for starting a revolution. I said what do you mean? He said he'd never seen a mixed crowd of one hundred or so people have so much fun in his life. Our *love* and *respect* for each other are off the charts, and we pray when others see us that they see *love* and *love* does not see color.

The Great Seven-Year Real Estate Collapse That Caused Bankruptcy

The fall I experienced from 2007–2014 was so brutally painful and a total dependence on God. Can you imagine having $2.1 million in savings and losing every dime of it, the fear of losing your home, all your automobiles, not providing for your family and the shame that goes along with it, not knowing if you will ever be able to make a living again, living life with little confidence? To this day, I really don't understand why God would allow so many good people to get hurt by the great recession— millions of people losing their life savings, homes, jobs, and so on.

It might be best to describe the events and come back to describe what it meant. Here's a little picture of what was lost. In 2006, I was building million-dollar homes in Gainesville in the subdivision of Marina Bay on Lake Lanier (four homes left I could not sell). I had thirteen townhomes at The Reserves at Ivy Creek (across the street from the Mall of Georgia), which did not sell. We had our own home in the subdivision on Grand Marina Circle along with a thirty-two-foot cabin cruiser boat, three $90,000 cars in the garage, and our personnel eight-thousand-square-foot residence in Dacula. There were about fifteen builders who came to the weekly builders meeting, and at the beginning of 2007, I was the only one still attending with the developer. Most builders have already given back their homes to the lenders. I was sitting on four homes that could not sell for the loan amount. I had a property in Dacula (mini horse ranch)(I'd sold the big horse ranch in 2004), four horses, house, and park-quality baseball field I'd built for my son, and a fishing pond. Along with ninety-three rental properties that I sold most off before the crash and had about fifteen left in inventory. At one point, it took me over $73,000 to get through the month (interest payments, maintenance, etc.) I held on till January 2010, went through a lot of savings, and could not sustain these payments anymore as real estate values continued to plummet. Now I got the joy of dealing with all the creditors coming after me for a couple of years, and on April 4, 2013, I had no alternative but to file for bankruptcy. Having religious convictions about debt, I tried to work payment plans with creditors, but at the end of the day, it became unreasonable.

At this point, I went through $1.3 million of hard-earned savings. The only creditor-exempt assets I had—so I thought—were an annuity with a surrender value of $582,000 (which I lost in a court ruling) and $215,000 in an IRA (won in a court ruling but exhausted to pay attorney fees and living expenses). Fighting for these two assets for eighteen months cost me over $100,000 in legal fees and gave me taste on how corrupt the legal system can be. I could write a book on this whole experience, but if anyone ever crosses this bridge, I am a legal expert on creditor-exempt assets, so feel free to ask.

Think about it for a moment: I set up a retirement annuity funded with after-tax dollars ten years before I filed for bankruptcy. I never touched the retirement account even in my darkest financial hour, because if I could hold on till I was 59.5 years old, the annuity would be worth $1.2 million. This was the only retirement program available for self-employed people. Judge Diehl ruled that because I exceeded the annual contribution limits (which apply to 401K and IRAs), the annuity was not creditor exempt. Then she went on to say that the Georgia law was "ambiguous" on the exemption. There was very little case law on this issue and none that applied to my self-employed status. I feel the judge gave the bankruptcy trustee a bone and me a bone and called it a day.

After the March 6, 2014, ruling, I went to one of the most reputable law firms in Atlanta on asset protection to appeal. After they did their research, they assured me I would have a good chance of winning on appeal and getting a bankruptcy discharge. They asked for a $10,000 retainer, which I thought would cover the appeal and my discharge. Six months later and $41,000 in additional legal fees, I ended up settling with the trustee and the only creditor to fight me was RES-GA. The settlement was that they would grant me my bankruptcy discharge if I gave up my entire annuity, which I did because my attorneys told me I'd have to post a 10 percent bond to appeal and legal fees would be another $100,000. Most importantly it was time to get a fresh start in life, and if God wanted me to start with nothing again, so be it. I was good with it. The biblical stories of Job and Joseph gave me strength and hope. Although this seemed very unjust, my faith has always prevailed.

Out of the dozens of creditors in my bankruptcy case, there was only one creditor that fought me, a private investment company called RES-GA. About 75 percent of my debt was to Haven Trust bank, which went bankrupt, and the FDIC was the receivership. RES-GA bought these assets for pennies on the dollar, made money on the purchase and sale, and came after me for the deficiency. How can triple dipping possibly be legal, especially when you are not even the original lender? And to make matters worse, RES-GA contested my bankruptcy discharge and was coming after me for the entire $2,446,748.14 I owed them.

The fix-and-flip and wholesaling sides of real estate investing were obsolete in 2010 as real estate values continued to decline. This forced me to find another means of making a living, so I entered the world of day-trading stocks in 2011. I bought all the books and tapes, did online study classes, and attended live seminars to learn the business. I had beginners luck and doubled my money the first sixty days, and I was hooked. Then in August 2011, the stock market made a correction like it had not seen since 1930s depression. It fell through four layers of support. Support is a price level that most of the time when the market corrects, it goes down to that price level and bounces back up. Most of my trades were either long call (up) or put (down) vertical spreads. I traded call and put options, which is a thousand times the leverage of buying one stock. So before the crash in July, the market was bullish (moving up). So when making a call-option trade, you want to follow a few basic rules:

1. Trade in the direction that the market is moving.
2. F/E (financial estimate) score of 3.25 or greater.
3. 250,000 average volume traded daily of the stock and most important.
4. Buy on support bounce and sell at resistance.
5. Expiration date at least thirty to sixty days out.

Prior to the crash, the market touched two levels of resistance (highest price point) and pulled back, and most analysis predicted that on the third attempt at resistance level it would break through for a major "breakout," as the market had in the past (technical analysis prediction). Sorry, Charlie; it did not work out that way. The market went up to resistance line and pulled back and reversed through support. Support is a price level on a stock chart where historically the stock has had difficulty falling below. The price level acts as a floor and prevents the price of the stock from falling any further.

When the market pulled back to support, I placed more trades as all the technical analysis suggested. I was basically following trading rules. So hopefully I painted a picture here of the trade not only going through one level of support but falling through four, and options trades having expiration dates approaching, none of my trades came to fruition, and I lost over $470,000. So here I was not making any income for two years, investing my life savings and losing it. I believe I was in line for either a stroke or a heart attack in September 2011 when my option expired and I lost every dime. I recall having dinner with my parents and siblings in Chicago on a family vacation; I picked up my phone to check my account, and I'd lost $78,000 that afternoon. My body was paralyzed. Hair was standing up on the back of my neck, and I thought I was going to have a heart attack.

You'd think I'd have had enough of day-trading stocks, but in October, I invested another $100,000, and I lost that by March 2012. You can't be successful in life without confidence, and I had very little, getting out of my trades prematurely, overtrading, trying to make up the losses and making fearful decisions. I don't think God wanted me married to my computer screen all day long, analyzing stock charts. It is a very secluded work environment and, being an extrovert, probably would not have been fulfilling as a lifelong career. Therefore, I felt God leading me back in real estate, and with the market finally bottoming out, it was good timing to get back into what I knew best and in which I had a successful track record.

On April 12, 2012, one of my fix-and-flip houses sold, which had been on the market for more than two years. This brought in some working capital. Although I lost $31,949 on the sale, it was money back into the bank account at the perfect time. Just to give you an example, this home sold for $69,900 in an area where homes had sold for $110,000 before 2008. Fate would have it that I had two other fix-and-flips in inventory also for two years that sold shortly after that with similar outcomes of losses of $27,165 and $30,761—great tax deductions if you are making money. But on a positive note, it was some operating capital. The crash forced me to reinvent myself and learn to fund projects by finding private money investors and joint-venture partnerships, and to do business with a set of new people. I had to build my reputation all over again due to most of the players being out of the business.

I understand the anxiety of going to the mailbox and having another creditor sue you, an abundance of legal problems, not being able to think straight because your heart is so heavy in fear. I remember driving my son, Michael, to practice with his friend in the car. My mind was so clouded that I passed the exit (which I'd been to a hundred times) and the boys looking at each other and saying, "Dad, what are you doing?"

So what does all this mean to me? Going through suffering and hardship? Losing all my money, dignity, pride and confidence? Going through a season of brokenness? God is in control over all things, and he is worthy of our worship, even though we may not understand what he is doing in our lives. Suffering is part of the human experience, and God allows suffering to enter our lives for a number of reasons: to test us (the testing of our faith develops perseverance) and to discipline us (all people, even the godliest among us, sin). God uses suffering to guide us back to his way when we stray, to humble us (pride is the fall of every man), to change our perspectives, and to prepare us for blessings in the future.

God alone is in sovereign control of all things. To think God has lost control or that he does not have our best interests at heart is to judge according to our human perspectives. When we do so, we fail to take God's perfect character into account. We are often too nearsighted to see the things God has in mind. God is far more concerned that we trust him than that we understand him since his ways and his wisdom far exceed our own.

> For I know the plans I have for you, declares the Lord,
> plans to prosper you and not to harm you, plans to give
> you hope and a future. (Jeremiah 29:11)

But seek first his kingdom and his righteousness, and all these things will be given to you as well. Therefore do not worry about tomorrow, for tomorrow will worry about itself. Each day has enough trouble of its own. (Matthew 6:33–34)

Love is patient and kind: love does not envy or boast: it is not arrogant or rude. It does not insist on its own way: it is not irritable or resentful: it does not rejoice at wrongdoing, but rejoices with the truth. Love bears all things, believes all things, hopes all things, and endures all things. Love never ends. Faith, hope and love abide, these three: but the greatest of these three is love. (1 Corinthians 13:4–8)

A cheerful heart is good medicine, but a crushed spirit dries up the bones. (Proverbs 17:22)

You need to understand the enemy is not really after your dreams, your health, or your finances. He's not primarily after your family. He's after your joy. The Bible says that "the joy of the LORD is your strength" (Nehemiah 8:10), and your enemy knows that if he can deceive you into living down in the dumps and depressed, you are not going to have the necessary strength—physically, emotionally, or spiritually—to withstand his attacks. When you rejoice in the midst of your difficulties, you're giving the enemy a black eye. He doesn't know what to do with people who keep giving God praise despite their circumstances. Learn how to smile and laugh. Quit being so uptight and stressed out. Make your choice to enjoy your life to the fullest today. Cast your cares upon the Lord, don't worry, release control and have joy in your heart no matter what the circumstance. One of God's comforts for me was "16" on the clock (John 3:16). I would look at the clock in the middle of the day, and it would read "1:16," or I would wake up at night at "3:16" in the morning. It was a way for God to comfort, saying, This all will soon pass.

I'm sure you've heard many stories of people going through adversity and saying, "It made me a better person." Well, what does that mean?

For me, it's having compassion and empathy for others, being patient with others, living a life of love, making at least three people a day smile. Arrogance and pride, we all fight these. I will never, ever brag about what I have and make someone else feel "less than." Stuff is nice, but at the end of the day, it does not mean anything. If God wants to allow wealth in my life again like before, I will treat that blessing a little humbler the next time around. I can give you dozens of examples of God's divine intervention during the past twenty years that have helped with my faith.

Feel free to reach out to me if I can be of encouragement to you and share my relationship with Christ with you.

ABOUT THE AUTHORS

Mike Cherwenka is known as the "Godfather of Fix-and-Flip" because he has flipped more than 2,100 homes. He also fosters real estate investors on their journeys to becoming experienced investors. Cherwenka teaches through a hands-on flipping experience.

Tolla Cherwenka started flipping luxury homes in upscale communities in Atlanta, Georgia, in 2005. Additionally, she is a worldwide thought leader and business-transformation architect for a Fortune 500 software company.

www.ingramcontent.com/pod-product-compliance
Lightning Source LLC
Chambersburg PA
CBHW071651210326
41597CB00017B/2182